LOVING OUR
DIFFERENCES

GEORGE SELIG, ED.D., & ALAN ARROYO, ED.D

LOVING OUR DIFFERENCES

BUILDING SUCCESSFUL FAMILY RELATIONSHIPS

PUBLISHING

Virginia Beach, Virginia

OUACHITA TECHNICAL COLLEGE

Be patient, bearing with
one another in love.
(Eph. 4:2 NIV)

ACKNOWLEDGMENTS

This book is dedicated to our wonderful and under-standing wives, Judy Selig and Susan Arroyo, as well as to our loving children: Cheryl Selig and Cynthia Towne; Andrew, David, Joseph, and Elisabeth Arroyo. Without their love, patience, encouragement, and support, this undertaking would not have been possible.

We would like to give special thanks to our friend, Cynthia Ellenwood, who edited our writing and provided supportive and insightful comments that we believe have added immeasurably to the quality and depth of this book.

Contents

Loving Our Differences

PROLOGUE

George Selig's Story

"I wish I was dead."

The woman's words startled me. It was not something I expected to hear at a church seminar on parenting. Her eyes had a telltale dullness about them. Her husband, standing beside her, was in obvious distress.

"She's been like this for some time," he said. "We can't seem to do anything to change the way she feels."

Oh no, I thought. What do I do now?

I had just started the seven-week series, and somehow I assumed everyone in the class would be fairly normal. My mind began to race as I tried to come up with counselors and psychologists trained to deal with serious depression.

"Have you thought of getting professional help?" I asked weakly.

"Yes, I have," she said, her voice almost devoid of emotion, "but nothing seems to help. I decided to come to your class because I thought that even if I can't feel good about life, I might at least try to be a better parent and a better wife."

My heart sank and I thought, "How can a course like mine do anything if you spend your entire day wishing you were dead?" Out loud I said as optimistically as I could, "Well, if you think you can handle the activities and weekly assignments, I'm certainly willing to help."

During the week as I prepared for the next class, all I could think about was that pathetic wife and husband and my inadequacies. I also thought about the sad condition of many other families in our country. Those people I had just met were not alone in their despair. With divorce rates running nearly fifty percent, abuse cases on the rise, financial strains forcing both parents to work, and a multitude of other sorrows, it seemed the institution of the family was being torn apart. Certainly most people weren't as upset as this couple, but a vast number were under extreme stress. Professional therapy for all of America's problem families were obviously not reasonable, yet what other solution was there?

I had been praying for the American family for years and searched for biblical principles that would help them, but sometimes I wondered if it were not too late to do much of anything. I was not convinced families like that could be salvaged or that I was the person to do it.

When I returned to teach my class the following week, the lady and her husband were back. They returned the next week and the next. As the course progressed, I thought I saw a change in her. She began to take more interest in her appearance. Occasionally she spoke up in class about problems she was having with her children and seemed to grasp how the principles could help her. I continued to pray daily for her and her family, but other than to say, "How are you doing?" I didn't broach the subject of her not wanting to live.

After the final class, the woman and her husband approached me. It was hard to believe this was the same person who had started the class. With sparkling eyes she said, "We want to thank you for this class. I feel better about myself than I've felt in years."

"It's true," said her husband. "She's happy and we both enjoy our children more than we ever did before."

"And they obey us without being threatened with a spanking all the time," she added with a smile. "I'm even keeping the house clean. I have time for myself and I know I'm a far better wife."

I was astonished. How could so much have occurred in such a short time? Then other families in the group began to come up. They, too, said the class had changed their lives, particularly their relationships with each other. Instead of quarreling over their differences, they had begun to love them. They were also excited about their ability to handle their parenting roles more effectively.

Over the next several months and years of using these materials, it dawned on me what had happened. It wasn't that I was a spectacular teacher. All I did was help them see how to apply the Bible to their personal lives. God gave parents sovereign authority over their homes, but in this age of permissive parenting and empty values they have lost control. With no confidence in themselves they have turned to secular experts to tell them about their children's personalities, their ability to achieve in school, and even the careers they should choose.

After taking these classes, husbands and wives not only began to take charge of their homes again, but they also learned how to talk to one another and live in harmony. They learned to understand one another's needs and respond to them.

As they began to try out various personality tests and understand the effects of immaturity on a person's attitudes and behavior, they were able to unlock mysteries that helped them build success into their families.

Although these principles are in the Bible, most of those who attended said they had never understood them before. The classes began a process that did not end with the completion of the sessions. It continued through the years. Even today, I hear from many of them how meaningful the course was and how it continues to make a difference in their lives. Not too long ago, I even saw the same woman who had once wanted to die—registering for a course at CBN University, where I am now dean of the College of Education and Human Services.

I am convinced after years of running successful parenting groups that most families don't need a therapist. They simply need to see one another as God sees them, each one with his unique needs and abilities.

Alan Arroyo's Story

They called them "at-risk" students. They were the

potential drop-outs, drug abusers, gang leaders, and pregnant teens. They were ready to give up on everything— first society, then themselves.

The teachers at this tough Illinois high school for turned-off kids were at-risk too— at-risk of losing their minds. Everything they had been taught that was supposed to motivate students didn't work. By the second week of school, one teacher had her resignation letter ready for delivery. Others were close to it.

As director of the program, it was my unfortunate responsibility (but unique opportunity) to find a way to motivate these young people and also save the sanity of my staff.

It was a vicious cycle for the kids. They didn't succeed because they weren't motivated, and they weren't motivated because they didn't succeed. How do you break in to that cycle? That was my dilemma.

I was in a tough spot until I recalled a book I had used a few months earlier with a parenting class at church. The book was by George Selig, a man I had never met nor heard of before. The book was unpretentious, but the compassionate way the author presented principles for understanding and helping children of all ages had caught my interest. Since the principles worked with the parents I taught on Sunday, maybe they would work at the Alternative High School.

The teachers were willing to try anything. They had a heart for the students but they didn't have a clue how to motivate them. I'll never forget the afternoon when I explained to them the concept that each person functions at a certain level of motivation. Regardless of their chronological age, the significant factor in understanding why people do what they do is their maturity level.

After a brief description of the four levels, light bulbs began to flash in their minds. Together we began to identify the level of motivation for each student in the school. Then we decided on the best academic and disciplinary strategies

4

to use for those at each level and prepared for a trial run.

Before he started using the concepts, Mr. Lewis's class thought math papers were something you used to reenact a dog fight over the Mediterranean. After he put the principles to work, for the first time most of his students completed their work and looked for more.

Before Mrs. James tried it, her students listened to her lecture for five minutes and spent the remainder of the class as nap time. After a week with the new strategy, students became so noisily involved in her class discussions that I raced down to the room to see what was happening. No problem. They were in good, old-fashioned, intellectual debate.

Discipline changed, too. Students knew that they all started at the lowest level, but the more they responded to the rules, the more responsibility and privileges they were given. They responded. Teachers learned quickly which approaches worked well for some and which were better for others.

Staff meetings were also different. Instead of spending our time complaining about this one or that one, we had a common framework to use for solving our problems.

Heaven? No, but in the words of one of the student's parents, "I never thought I would see Adrian turned-on about anything, much less school."

Later that year, state officials came to visit the program. Student attendance, grades, and attitudes were vastly improved. Was it for real? After the visit, one state official said, "This is one of the best programs I have seen to help kids stay in school— and in life!"

After years of working with special and at-risk youth, I had an opportunity to move to CBN University in Virginia Beach, Virginia, to teach graduate students these educational principles along with George Selig, the author of the book that had transformed the high school. When they heard the principles, the graduate students with previous teaching experience asked us, "Where have these ideas been? I wish I'd had these principles to work with fifteen years ago." One student, returning from his internship, remarked, "When I used these concepts with two problem children, I saw their motivation for academics improve dramatically. Their relationships with the other teachers and me became a strong bond."

As you read this book, you will find a number of stories about how people discovered these principles and put them into practice. Details of the stories have been fictionalized for reason of privacy and some are composites, but they all represent what happened when families decided to give God first place in their lives and to love one another— differences and all— as much as they loved themselves.

We have also included a number of family activities to help you discover your gifts and differences. You will find them in the appendix/packet and may also purchase a separate packet that is easy for children and adults to follow.

We can't pretend that one book could ever be a cure-all for every family. However, it is our prayer that this book will be a blessing to your family, and that you will become one of the growing number of success stories in America, instead of one of the unneccessary failures. As God told the Israelites, "Be strong and very courageous; be careful to do according to all the law which Moses My servant commanded you; do not turn from it to the right or to the left, so that you may have success wherever you go" (Josh. 1:7 NASB).

CHAPTER ONE

GROWING STAGES

I left the house this morning praising the Lord. That spirit of elation lasted until I reached the freeway. From out of nowhere, a car cut across two lanes of traffic; leaning on his horn, the driver cut in front of me. From out of nowhere, rage cut into me, and I found myself beating on my horn, shouting, "You stupid idiot! Why don't you watch where you're going?"

My 17-year-old daughter on the edge of her seat beside me said, "Dad, what he did was wrong, but you didn't give a very good witness."

The first thought in my hot head was to tell her to be quiet, but then I woke up to reality. I had blown it again.

"You're right," I said. "I'm sorry."

After I dropped her off at school and continued on to work, I thought soberly about the morning's events. When I left the house, I had felt like a man of God. All I wanted was to do His will. Twenty minutes later, I acted like a child. All I wanted was revenge. In a matter of seconds I had a perfect example of something I have been teaching for years: the motivational levels of human beings.

Motivational Levels

Motivational levels are the stages we pass through on the road to maturity. At each level, we make decisions based on certain needs, goals, and desires. Sometimes we reach a new level only to slip backwards when new circumstances arise, but we should continue striving upward, reaching beyond ourselves to serve God and man.

Young children, and sometimes adults in traffic, are motivated primarily by the need for self-gratification. This is what we call **Level 1**— the *me* level.

Level 2 is often called the *approval* level. These individuals have progressed beyond simple self-gratification and are beginning to seek approval from others, especially those who are important in their lives.

Level 3 is the *personal relationship* level. People at this level have a desire to be seen as competent. They seek respect and desire relationships with others based on mutual acceptance and trust.

Level 4 is the *others-oriented* level of behavior. For a Christian, this means love and obedience to God, and loving others as you love yourself. These individuals have a servant's heart—reaching out with no thought of reciprocity or reward.

The process of moving from self-centeredness to God-centeredness is described in the Bible as sanctification. When a child is born, it is only natural for him to be self-centered and demanding, motivated by immediate needs that must be met. As he matures, however, his motivation changes focus and he desires to meet others' needs. Finally, he finds that he wants to please God.

Christians who function at Level 4 are demonstrating an unqualified commitment to Christ. Many good people who are not Christians operate at this level in some areas of their lives, but only Christ can enable someone to be consistently self-sacrificing in every area. No other gods can grant that kind of power.

Family Discipleship

Survival training for marriage should include lessons on the levels of motivation. When one partner pushes the other's "hot button" and triggers an emotional outburst, he is causing that person to regress to motivational Level 1, the self-protection stage. That should not be. Instead of playing such immature games, couples should learn how to disciple one another toward growth. In the process, they will also find it easier to disciple their children.

In contrast to their parents, children are not being sinful when they operate for several years at lower levels of motivation. "Foolishness is bound up in the heart of a child" (Prov. 22:15), but that doesn't make them hopelessly "bad." It simply means that they need patient discipleship with extra structure, love, and encouragement to help them progress to the next level. The Level 1 label does not define worth, nor does it imply that God loves someone any less. It just identifies someone who is trying to meet his own needs because he does not have the faith or maturity to trust that God will meet them. He still responds more to his carnal nature than to God. Parents have the opportunity to help their child— God's precious gift— to become all that God desires him to be.

There was a time when, I must admit, I dreaded going to church. It wasn't because I didn't like the preaching or the music. I just didn't like the sideshow going on in front of me.

Every Sunday we seemed to sit directly behind Billy, a six-year-old boy who was an absolute handful for his parents. The chairs in the sanctuary were the folding type used in theaters. During the singing, Billy always climbed up on his seat. I tried to sing, but I couldn't help watching for the inevitable to happen. About halfway through the choruses, *Wham!* Billy's seat would fold up, nearly guillotining his leg. There would be outcries of pain, then hugs, an outpouring of cuddling and consolation, then absolute freedom for Billy to spend the rest of the service doing whatever he wanted.

Occasionally, Billy's father would decide the boy had gone too far and try to exercise his authority. Like a shot, Billy would scurry to the mother's side. If his father persisted, Billy's mother would put her finger to her mouth and say "Shsssh" to her husband. "You're disturbing the people behind us," she would say in a stage whisper. As I watched this scenario, I kept hoping the father would win the battle. Billy always seemed far more disruptive than his father ever hoped to be. Billy's antics eventually drew the attention of the pastor, but when he spoke to the parents, Bill and Toni, he was met with denial, excuses, and sometimes even anger.

Billy's parents couldn't cope with him because they had no understanding of the different maturity levels of children. They were bright parents, both young professionals, but they were trying to control him with the kind of gentle persuasion that only works at higher levels of motivation. They felt so bad about their failure that they reacted to the pastor as I did in a traffic jam. Even though they functioned at Level 3 or 4 in most areas of their lives, they dropped to Level 1 when confronted. This made it impossible for the pastor to have a constructive conversation with them.

A Success Story

One day when I happened to be speaking with them, Bill asked, "Didn't you write a book on parenting?" I responded that I had written one several years ago. Then he asked, "Could I talk to you about Billy?"

My heart should have leaped for joy, but knowing the experience of the pastor and others I thought, "Oh, no. I don't want to get into this." Quite honestly, I had developed a slight visceral dislike for the entire family because they had so often disturbed my opportunity to worship the Lord.

Almost instantly, I felt a sting of conviction over my bad attitude. At the Holy Spirit's urging I took a fresh look at the father. Instead of a thorn in my side, I saw a human being in need. Asking the Lord's forgiveness, I began to listen.

As we talked, he told me that he had read several books on parenting but nothing seemed to work. When I heard the strategies he described, I realized he had been trying to use one of the typical methods that assume a child is at a maturity level of 3 or 4. The authors of this kind of child-rearing book assume that every child can carry on an adult-level conversation, carefully expressing his feelings about why he is misbehaving.

There is nothing wrong with such a strategy when the child is motivated to build relationships (Level 3) or desires to serve others without reward (Level 4). For a Level 1 child, however, such a strategy is almost hopeless.

I asked the father if he wanted me to help him find techniques that might work. With a trace of desperation in his voice he responded, "We have to do something or it's going to tear our marriage and family apart. The house is becoming like an armed camp."

The next evening, in Bill and Toni's home, I offered them a simple explanation to their problem that would eventually transform their lives. I told them that as each child grows, he changes not only in a physical sense but also in his responses to the world around him. He passes through four basic levels of motivation that correspond to these stages of spiritual growth described in Scripture:

Level 1 is the Baby Stage (1 Cor. 3:1-4).
Level 2 is the Little Child Stage (1 John 2:12).
Level 3 is the Young Man Stage (1 John 2:13).
Level 4 is the Father Stage (1 John 2:13).

The Apostle Paul wrote in the "love chapter" of 1 Corinthians 13: "When I was a child, I spoke as a child, I thought as a child, I reasoned as a child." He was saying that adults and children don't think alike. They respond to different urges. They are motivated differently.

Until recently, except for biblical references like those mentioned, Christians have paid scant attention to stages of human growth and development. Secular theorists, however, have been busy trying to understand it. I explained a few of these theories to Bill and Toni.

One of the most well-known theorists on this subject, Abraham Maslow, described a hierarchy of five maturity levels. At the lowest level, people are happy as long as someone can constantly meet their physiological needs like food and sleep. As they mature, Maslow said, they are progressively motivated by the need for safety, then social relationships, then esteem by others and, ultimately, self-actualization.

Although some elements of Maslow's theory have validity, there are problems. Research has not supported his assumption that all five needs exist in everyone, nor that the needs are met in the order he proposed. Most important, his ultimate goal of self-actualization is self-centered, not God-centered. It implies some responsibility for others, but includes no motive to please God. Maslow, an unbeliever, also denied the power of God to sovereignly raise individuals up out of the lowest levels and transform them into a new creation.

Secular models like those of Maslow, Clayton Alderfer, and Lawrence Kohlberg operate under two assumptions:

1. Meet your own needs first.
2. To your own self be true.

The Bible tells us,
"Seek ye first the kingdom of God . . .
and all these things [basic needs]
shall be added unto you" (Matt. 6:33 KJV).

12

Reaching Children At Their Level

I explained to Billy's parents that a child operating at a certain motivational level is not "bad" any more than an infant is "bad" when he demands that someone feed him. Although he may sin, he is still created in God's image. Jesus died for Billy so that he could be redeemed and mature in Christ's image.

As parents, they should expect to fulfill their child's basic needs during his early years. If they do not, he will be delayed in the normal process of outgrowing those needs. When such a child does grow, he is more likely to regress quickly under stress.

Newborn babies and toddlers won't progress beyond motivational Levels 1 and 2, but that does not make them less lovable. It simply means that parents will have to give them more attention, love, and direction than at later stages. When the child is ready, parents begin to impose limits on his demands so that he can grow.

From infancy to adolescence, a child's carnal nature is constantly rebelling against the maturing process. Good discipleship from his parents can keep these forces from pushing him back to lower levels where self-gratification and peer approval once again rule his life. A child who has never received proper *external* controls from parents has difficulty developing *internal* controls. He becomes easy prey for a society increasingly dedicated to the self.

Children lose respect for their parents when they do not receive the structure they need to help them grow. This disrespect is fed by a diet of films and television programs depicting fathers and mothers as inept and constantly outsmarted by their tremendously intelligent and "with-it" children. Flip answers and verbal challenges inevitably follow. The rapid increase in drugs and immorality among teenagers can be stopped if there is a revival in parental discipleship and a refusal to allow these negative stereotypes to be perpetuated.

Restoring the Discipleship of Children

The first step in reversing this process of deterioration is for parents to get to know their children. I asked Bill and Toni to complete a behavior checklist on Billy to see which motivational level described him best. Here is a sampling of the way they described him:

When they finished and did the computations, it was clear that Billy operated generally on Level 2, except when his parents dared to oppose his behavior. Then he regressed obstinately to Level 1. Looking over the checklist, I explained as gently as I could, "What you need to do, if you expect his behavior to change, is to stop treating him as an adult and trying to reason with him. His regression when you try to correct him proves that he has not reached a motivational level where gentle persuasion is effective. He needs you both to resume authority over his behavior and give him clear direction and structure so he can finish with Level 1 and move on."

Toni said with concern, "I'm afraid he'll grow up without a mind of his own if we structure his life for him. Won't he become too dependent on adult authority?"

I responded, "Toni, if you don't structure Billy now, he'll have a hard time accepting limits on his behavior from anyone for the rest of his life. No one will want to be around him. Let me give you an example. Have you ever entertained a family in your home who let their child do anything and touch everything, even your valuable knickknacks and sentimental items that could never be replaced?"

Bill and Toni looked uncomfortable, but knowing their great need, I continued, "These people usually ignore their child's behavior, or say weakly, 'Please don't touch.' If he does it anyway, they just ignore him."

"When that happens in my house, I usually have to speak to the child myself. If he persists, I put the item out of his reach. By the time the family leaves, I'm angry because they didn't discipline their child, and I decide never to invite

BILLY'S MOTIVATIONAL INVENTORY CHECKLIST
(Number 5 means "most of the time," number 3 means "sometimes," and number 1 means "rarely or never.")

Score

1. He/she wants his own way. — 1 2 3 4 ⑤
2. He/she will say,"Hey, look at me!" — 1 2 3 4 ⑤
3. He/she will do most tasks if verbally praised for his efforts. — 1 2 3 ④ 5
4. He/she is known by my friends as somewhat of a "show-off." — 1 2 3 ④ 5
5. He/she has a very short attention span and changes activities often. — 1 2 3 ④ 5
6. He/she frequently says, "No, that's mine!" — 1 2 ③ 4 5
7. He/she will play with others' toys without asking. — 1 2 3 ④ 5
8. He/she will become angry and throw a temper tantrum if he does not get what he wants immediately. — 1 2 3 ④ 5
9. He/she demands that his achievements be placed on display for others to admire. — 1 2 3 4 ⑤
10. He/she enjoys participating in competitive activities, but is upset if his efforts are not recognized. — 1 2 3 4 ⑤
11. He/she will behave most appropriately when attention is centered on him. — 1 2 3 4 ⑤
12. He/she will lose interest in an activity if someone is not there watching and encouraging him. — 1 2 3 4 ⑤
13. He/she will become interested in certain subjects, activities, or hobbies in order to win approval. — 1 2 3 4 ⑤
14. He/she becomes unusually upset when others disagree with him. — 1 2 3 ④ 5
15. He/she must be told specifically what I expect him to do before he is able to comply. — 1 2 3 ④ 5

them back unless they come alone. Relationships with our friends have become strained after episodes like that. It always makes me sad to lose a friendship and also to see a child embarking on such a destructive course."

"As the years pass, parents who have avoided imposing structure on their children when they were young often have problems when they enter school. Beginning in kindergarten they get reports from teachers that little Julie or

Johnny refuses to settle down and learn. Later, they find that their teenagers have trouble keeping part-time jobs and sometimes get involved with alcohol and drugs. If they go to college, they flunk out or get involved in activities not at all pleasing to the Lord."

Toni said, "I've known kids who turned out like that whose parents were very strict, not permissive."

"You're right," I answered. "Some parents establish close structure and strict discipline early, but they don't know when to stop. Even when their children grow up and advance to higher levels of motivation, the parents continue to treat them as though they were at Level 1. In time that, too, causes rebellion."

"These overly disciplined children seem to respond in two ways. They either regress to the parents' level of expectation, which is Level 1, or they become very passive and pretend to be obedient. When they reach adolescence, however, they often act out all the rebellion they have been building up for years."

"We've sensed that some of our friends seemed to be distancing themselves from us, haven't we?" Bill said to his wife. "They haven't come right out and said it, but I'm afraid their coldness probably comes from the way Billy acts in their homes."

"The other alternative of too much structure doesn't sound very good either," said Toni.

I nodded agreement. "What I recommend is that you structure your discipline in a way that meets Billy's individual needs. As soon as he grows in maturity, you can give him more independence and more input into decisions that affect him. When he reaches Level 3 or 4, you'll be able to discipline him the way you do now, but only because you have trained him in the first place. For now, you have to use external controls to help him develop internal controls. That's consistent with Proverbs 22:6: 'Train up a child in the way he should go: and when he is old, he will not depart from it.'"

Toni was still not quite convinced. "I'm afraid that if we

start to make more demands on him, Billy will think we don't love him," she admitted.

"Toni," I said, "which do you think is a greater act of love— allowing Billy to run his life before he's equipped or taking charge temporarily until he has the necessary skills?"

"Well, obviously the second, but I'm concerned about how Billy will react," Toni said.

She looked so earnest that I had to laugh. As a parent, I have been through the resistance myself. "Billy will definitely give you a hard time at first," I said with a grin, "but ask the Lord to give you more persistence than your son, and pretty soon it will start to taper off. When he finds out that you're not going to budge, he'll settle down."

"No child truly wants to run his life alone. Even though they demand freedom, deep down inside, children want security and protection. Immature children who are allowed to run their lives become restless and easily agitated because they're afraid of being in total control but don't understand those feelings. When they finally accept the authority of their parents, they become much happier and more peaceful."

I gave Bill and Toni three keys to successful parenting: *Know, Grow,* and *Sow.*

Know your child. Adapt yourself to him. Everything you do to help him mature should be individually keyed to his motivational level and personality.

Grow along with your child. Adjust your training techniques up and down as the child fluctuates in maturity.

Sow good seed for the future. Work together with your spouse to develop a long-range plan for his growth.

When God gave Moses the Fourth Commandment, "Honor thy father and thy mother: that thy days may be long in the land which the Lord thy God giveth thee" (Ex. 20:12 KJV), he was establishing a primary principle for the family: obedience to proper authority results in peaceful hearts and minds which are essential ingredients of the abundant life that God offers to all His people.

Bill and Toni felt guilty about Billy, but I told them that

parenting is one of the hardest jobs in the world, and nobody does it perfectly. The important thing is to be open to change when God shows you the way. Also, they needed to remember that eventually Billy will have to account to God for his behavior.

We prayed for God's forgiveness for two well-meaning parents and for Bill and Toni to forgive one another. Then we asked God for His assistance in re-establishing His authority in their house and Bill and Toni's authority over Billy. By now the hour was getting late, so I gave them some suggestions for putting to work the concepts of Know, Grow, and Sow:

Set goals for one month, three months, and a year. They must be in agreement about those goals, or they would once again become a house divided. Included in this plan would be an expectation that Billy would take increased responsibility for his behavior and do household chores suitable to his age.

Search your own hearts. I encouraged them to discover their level of motivation as they related to Billy and to each other. When parents become frustrated with their children and react at Level 1, their actions may stop misbehavior temporarily, but angry outbursts offer no positive opportunity for instruction or encouragement. It is like the unclean spirit that was driven out of the house but returned, bringing even more wicked spirits, because nothing had been done to fill the house with light (Matt. 12:43-45). Punishment that is not followed with loving instruction and encouragement does not bear good fruit.

Establish a family devotion time every day. One of the best ways to help children grow out of the self-centered stage is to center them on God. Parents should read aloud Bible stories that depict positive character qualities like obedience, trust, and forgiveness. Children need to see that blessings come with obedience. They also need time to receive their parents' loving instruction when they are not being disciplined for their sins. This time does not have to be a "church" type ceremony. Ideas for real life devotions and lessons will be given in later chapters.

Pray together, being careful to pray *for* your children and not *at* them. Some people use prayer as a tool for sending barbed messages, not a means of communicating with God.

I had other sessions with Bill and Toni, covering subjects that you will find in future chapters of this book. They learned how to determine Billy's spiritual gifts and to understand how his personality affected every area of his life. They had an opportunity to improve their communication with Billy and with one another. They saw how character development is related to spiritual growth and how to build Billy's self-esteem. Instead of seeing household chores as a punishment for Billy, they learned how to use them to help him grow. The principles also gave them a basis for talking to Billy's teacher at school and improving his performance there.

Billy did test his parents, as I knew he would, but because they had decided to keep a unified and loving front, they held firm. In a short time, Billy became more obedient and respectful. From a personal standpoint, I can tell you that Billy became a joy to sit behind in church. But, wouldn't you know, Bill's company transferred him about three months later, so I missed seeing the continued progress that he made.

So far, God has not placed me behind any more Billys in church, but I have heard about quite a few of them through my seminars and classes. Many of these have also become a joy to their parents when corrective action was taken, consistent with biblical principles.

I would encourage readers of this book to complete the checklist that Billy's family used so that you can get an accurate assessment of each child's current motivational level. You will find it in the appendix/packet. I would also encourage you to complete the checklist on yourself, being as honest as you can. If your marriage is strong, open, and forgiving, you can even complete one on each other. If you are not yet ready to do that, finish reading the book first.

As your understanding grows, you may become more willing to talk openly and find ways to help each other. Incompatibilities become a problem of the past when we use the tools God has given us to build bridges. You will read about one of these power tools in the following chapter.

CHAPTER TWO

GOD'S GOOD GIFTS

"Joanna, come down here!" shouted Dan as he strode in the front door.

In the upstairs bedroom, Dan's wife heard his calls with a twinge of pain. She thought bitterly, "Is he going to start that fight again?" Unconsciously she straightened her back and stiffened her jaw. "God, you know that I'm sick and tired of having him criticize me and the children. If he doesn't stop all that condemnation soon . . ."

She let her thoughts trail off as she stepped cautiously down the stairs. Dan was already out of sight. She could hear him banging around in the kitchen.

"Joanna!" he called again.

"What is it you want?" she asked testily as she walked into the kitchen.

To her surprise, Dan was smiling, and rather sheepishly at that. He walked over and took both of her hands. Looking into her eyes with more love than she had seen for a long time he said, "Can you forgive me for the way I've been treating you?" Joanna didn't know what to say, so she let him continue. "I finally realized how harsh and judgmental I've been with you and the children."

Joanna's eyes were starting to brim with tears so he hurried on. "What I discovered tonight was that God gave you and me different gifts. We have a different perspective on things. You look at a situation one way and I look at it another way. I've been condemning you for not seeing the world the way I see it. I've been making myself the model for what is 'right' and disparaging anyone who didn't see things my way. I need to listen more to what you say."

"You have something to offer me," he said, his words tumbling out, tripping over one another. "I see things as hard and fast, black and white, right and wrong, so I spout off as though I just came off Mount Sinai with the Ten Commandments under my arm."

He looked so earnest that for the first time in years he seemed to Joanna almost childlike. He kept searching her eyes for a response, and suddenly Joanna felt like laughing. It was wonderful! Her prayers for God to soften Dan's heart had finally had an effect on him. As she began to laugh and cry, Dan joined her and they clung to one another in the sheer joy of reconciliation and understanding. As soon as she caught her breath, Joanna asked excitedly, "What in the world has happened to you?"

Instead of answering immediately, Dan said, "I wanted to fix you some tea, but I couldn't find where you keep the tea bags."

Joanna laughed again. She had always been the one to wait on him. "They're in the cabinet over the stove," she said, sitting down at the kitchen table.

It was hard for her to believe that this was happening to her. She knew that Dan had attended a church seminar that evening on something called the "functional gifts," but she had no idea what that meant. It had something to do with the Bible, so Dan had decided to go. He was always trying to improve his mind. "This time he really did," she thought as she chuckled to herself.

Over tea Dan began to explain what he had learned. "The teaching was from the twelfth chapter of Romans," he said, pulling out his Living Bible. "Let me read you the first couple of verses. It says, 'I plead with you to give your bodies to God. Let them be a living sacrifice, holy—the kind he can accept. When you think of what he has done for you, is this too much to ask?'"

He looked up at his wife. "That's reasonable, right?" Joanna nodded, and he continued, "When I accepted Jesus Christ as Savior, I gave Him lordship over my life. At least I thought I did. I said, 'Take all of me, Lord,' but unconsciously I held back. I didn't take inventory of who I am, so I didn't even know that I wasn't giving Him all of me. Tonight I took a test that showed me a lot more about who I am and who you are, and I made up my mind to give the rest of myself to Christ."

Joanna was sipping her tea and trying not to giggle. She was waiting, praying silently, thankfully. Dan picked up the Bible again. "Here's the next verse," he said. " 'Don't copy the behavior and customs of this world, but be a new and different person with a fresh newness in all you do and think. Then you will learn from your own experience how his ways will really satisfy you.'"

"You haven't been satisfied with me lately, but I haven't been satisfied with me, either. I was getting frustrated trying to make everyone do things my way. I didn't understand that we aren't all supposed to see things the same way."

"Here's another verse farther down where Paul is talking about the body of Christ: 'We each have different work to do. So we belong to each other, and each needs all the others.'"

Joanna interrupted, "Those verses say to me that our family and the church have different types of people in them because God made it that way. When we don't like the differences we see in others and try to change them, the family is upset, we're frustrated, and so is God. He can't work out His plan for us."

"That's right!" Dan said excitedly. "I thought I was making the family conform to God's plan by correcting you and the children all the time. I thought it was my responsibility to straighten out all of you, but the standard I was using was myself instead of God's standard. I was trying to change you in a worldly way, 'in the flesh,' so to speak, by forcing my opinions on you."

"I'm afraid the same applies to me, too," Joanna admitted quietly. "I know I've been too easy on the children sometimes. I was so convinced that you were wrong that I thought I should make up for your strictness with a little leniency. I justified letting them get away with things by pretending I was being the nicer parent, but I'm afraid I was just trying to get even with you." She paused. "Can you forgive me?"

"Of course," Dan said with emotion. "Neither one of us could see what was going on. God wants us to start looking at life in a new way, to be transformed by renewing our minds from the inside so we can see things the way He sees them. It doesn't matter if a few sparks fly between us. 'Iron sharpens iron.'"

"O.K.," Joanna said with a grin. "So who did you discover that you are, and who am I?"

Understanding the Functional Gifts

Dan's class had covered a subject that several Christian teachers and authors have approached in recent years—using the list of gifts in Romans 12 to help people understand and appreciate individual differences. It is a much-needed subject. Christians are far too critical of one another.

Sometimes they seem even worse than their worldly counter-parts because they judge one another with such self-right-eous zeal.

Seven gifts are listed in Romans 12 and each one is related to the way an individual functions in a group. These functional gifts are Prophecy, Service, Teaching, Exhorta-tion, Giving, Leadership, and Mercy.

The chapters that precede this listing deal mostly with God's relationship with man— His love, His grace, His power, His presence. In the twelfth chapter, Paul explained that God gave gifts to believers so they could serve one another, and in so doing demonstrate the characteristics of the Giver. Individuals in a group like a family or church should be able to look around at the other members and praise God for the rich variety of gifts among His people.

Unfortunately, instead of praising God for their differ-ences, people often disparage others who are not like them-selves. That was what happened to Dan and Joanna, and it happens every day in the church. The cause of this dishar-mony is pride. It is evidence of spiritual immaturity and ignorance of the truth.

These problems can be solved. An important step is to "clothe yourselves with humility toward one another, be-cause God opposes the proud but gives grace to the humble" (1 Pet. 5:5 NIV). Dan did this symbolically when he prepared tea for his long-suffering wife. The Romans 12 passage compares submission to God with the Old Testament prac-tice of placing sacrifices on the altar. Christians are to be living sacrifices, submitting their minds as well as their bodies, allowing God to transform them according to His will.

Another step is to learn the truth about yourself and others and respect them as individuals. They, too, are made in the image of God, but they reflect a different part of His likeness. Dan discovered the truth through a class and gift inventory test. At the end of the chapter you will have an opportunity to fill one out as well.

Everyone is born with the gifts described in Romans

12, but they remain latent until he is born again and the Spirit can empower them. Without the work of the Holy Spirit, the person often remains at the lower motivational levels where his or her gift is dominated by the natural, fleshly nature. In those instances, the person becomes more of a liability to his family or church than an asset.

This chapter will show you the picture of each gift at its best (when the Holy Spirit controls it) and at its worst (when it is dominated by the fleshly human nature).

Remember that the levels of motivation can also reflect spiritual development. At higher levels of motivation, the gifts will be expressed in a more Christ-like and Spirit-controlled way. At the lower levels of motivation, the gifts will show more fleshly characteristics.

The Gift of Giving

Included in the gift list of Romans 12 is Giving. Individuals with an inborn gift of Giving are less common than those with the other functional gifts. There are examples of unbelieving philanthropists who give generously to social causes, but only God provides the momentum to enable individuals to give at all times, even when they have nothing to spare. Giving is a "spiritual temperature" gift that indicates how closely an individual is submitted to God.

GIFT OF GIVING	
GIVING AT ITS BEST	GIVING AT ITS WORST
Generous	Manipulative
Loving	Stubborn
Helpful	Unsubmitting
Careful	Undisciplined

Other Gifts and the Gift Dimensions

The other six gifts listed in Romans 12 affect the following activities: evaluating a situation, telling others about it, and taking action. We call these categories *appraisal, instruction*, and *results*.

The gifts of Prophecy and Mercy guide the way an individual *appraises* a situation and, as Dan and Joanna found out, they represent two extremes. Until they could understand one another's perspective, Dan and Joanna's differences made their lives miserable. Without God's intervention, they could have been on the way to divorce, and yet the solution was so simple. Here is a summary of each gift.

APPRAISAL GIFTS	
PROPHECY AT ITS BEST	PROPHECY AT ITS WORST
Analytical	Arrogant
Honest	Opportunistic
Biblical	Inflexible
Bold	Critical
Repentant	Hurtful
MERCY AT ITS BEST	MERCY AT ITS WORST
Sensitive	Resentful
Kind	Weak in discipline
Protective	Self-pitying
Reconciliating	Acting like a martyr

The gifts of Teaching and Exhortation guide an individual's preferred style of *instruction*. Those with the gift of Teaching tend to be patient and conscious of details. Those with the gift of Exhortation make demands that challenge their students to excel.

INSTRUCTIONAL GIFTS	
TEACHING AT ITS BEST	TEACHING AT ITS WORST
Patient	Sarcastic
Diligent	Disorganized
Reliable	Anxious
Clear	Careless

INSTRUCTIONAL GIFTS	
EXHORTATION AT ITS BEST	EXHORTATION AT ITS WORST
Persuasive	Self-promoting
Inspiring	Shallow
Spiritual	Worldly
Committed	Apathetic

The gifts of Leadership and Service affect how someone tries to get *results*. Those with the gift of Leadership prefer to get results by coordinating the work of others. Those with the gift of Service prefer to pitch in and do it themselves.

RESULTS GIFTS	
LEADERSHIP AT ITS BEST	LEADERSHIP AT ITS WORST
Visionary	Insecure
Stable	Paranoid
Effective	Overbearing
Prayerful	Self-centered
SERVICE AT ITS BEST	SERVICE AT ITS WORST
Flexible	Reluctant
Sensitive	Insensitive
Joyful	Isolated
Caring	Self-pitying

As you can see, when a family or church has a number of individuals operating at low motivational levels, it will suffer from constant dissension. The solution is not to break up the group, however. It is to initiate loving, prayerful discipleship of these individuals until they grow to higher levels of maturity. Without love, said Paul, the gifts are worth nothing.

A group needs to love and assist its members because they are important to God and their gifts are needed to make the group complete. One of the greatest mistakes is to label those who operate differently from oneself as "bad" or "wrong." Although individuals can misuse their gifts at lower levels of motivation, all God's gifts are good. Some methods are more effective in one situation, and other methods more effective in others, but God intends for all His people to mature and put His gifts to work.

The following is a more detailed examination of the gifts and how they affect the activities of adults. Later in this chapter is a description of signs of gifts that appear in children. After reading this chapter, discover the gifts of each person by taking the test in the appendix/packet.

Appraising Situations with Eyes of Prophecy

In the opening story, Dan told Joanna that he had finally recognized how different they were and decided to accept her as herself. That is something that every family, church, and organization needs to do. Dan didn't realize it, but he had been using his gift of Prophecy at a low motivational level. He had somewhat childishly insisted that his viewpoint was right and criticized those who saw things differently. When he accepted the validity of his wife's Mercy-oriented appraisal style, he was on his way to maturity.

Those with a gift of Prophecy view every situation in terms of absolutes—right and wrong, black and white. At their best they rationally analyze each proposal, rejecting anything unscrupulous. They insist on absolute truth, using the Bible instead of personal preferences to judge themselves and others. In a crisis, they may require "repentance and removal" of anyone caught in a sinful practice and are willing to confess their own sin when confronted with it.

Of course, they are not always at their best. When they are operating at a lower motivational level they may choose short-term gain over principle, become arrogant and domineering, and overstate their judgments to the point of deception. Sometimes they are so inconsiderate that they leave a trail of hurting people behind them.

An organization without a prophet is ultimately an

organization without a conscience, but a prophet gone awry can be disruptive and even dangerous. The mass suicide of Jonestown bears witness to the worst example in recent memory of a Christian leader with the gift of Prophecy.

Since then, we have seen other leaders fall, partly due to their self-appointed conviction that what they do is always right. They rely on isolated Bible verses or concentrate only on certain areas of life, not integrating everything into a meaningful whole.

You have already read about Dan and Joanna and the problems of church leaders. Here is an example of what can happen in the business world.

Tim was a senior accountant at a small firm. Although he was a Christian who was generally liked by the junior accountants he supervised, Tim had a reputation for tolerating no miscalculations or missed deadlines. The employees lived in fear of making mistakes because he appraised each error, regardless of its seriousness, as a major lapse. This attitude destroyed staff morale and resulted in frequent turnover.

Finally, one of the junior accountants took Tim aside and pointed out what was occurring. Tim broke quickly. He was aware that something was wrong but had never seen that his adherence to unreasonable standards was out of balance. Following the conversation, he made every effort to change and even went so far as to ask forgiveness of all those he had offended. In addition, he asked the junior accountant to alert him when his methods became rigid again. Within six months, the company had been transformed. The junior accountants began to do superior work, not because they were constantly berated but because they knew they were respected by Tim.

Appraising Situations with Eyes of Mercy

Joanna, the woman in the opening story, had a strong gift of Mercy, which for the first part of her married life left her at odds with her husband. After they both became aware of their different gifts, they didn't suddenly see everything eye-to-eye but they learned not to take their opposite perspectives as personal affronts. When they started listening to one another life became more pleasant for the entire family.

Those with a gift of Mercy tend to consider proposals more as entire units than as individual details. They appraise life with the heart more than the mind. They are so sensitive to people that they know almost immediately if someone is experiencing joy or pain and try to help, even when it is not socially acceptable. In a conflict, they try to bring about forgiveness.

At lower motivational levels, those with the gift of Mercy sometimes develop a "martyr complex," building resentment over perceived slights. They may engage in self-pity. Parents with the gift of Mercy may have difficulty bringing order into their children's lives.

Jesus was often confronted by those who had a disdain for the gift of Mercy. Religious leaders criticized Him for healing on the Sabbath and for reaching out to "publicans and sinners."

It will always be difficult for those with the gift of Prophecy to understand the need for Mercy, but only at lower levels of motivation will they refuse to reach out for it. As Shakespeare wrote in *The Merchant of Venice*,

> *The quality of mercy is not strain'd,*
> *It droppeth as the gentle rain from heaven*
> *Upon the place beneath. It is twice bless'd:*
> *It blesseth him that gives and him that takes.*
> *'Tis mightiest in the mightiest: it becomes*
> *The throned monarch better than his crown . . .*
> *It is an attribute to God himself;*
> *And earthly power doth then show likest God's*
> *When mercy seasons justice.*

Teaching Style of Instruction

From the time children are born, they begin a learning process that will last a lifetime. They will be taught by parents and grandparents, church and school teachers, preachers and friends. In many ways, the person they become will be affected by the instructional style of each one of these teachers. In turn, most children will, in some areas of their lives, become instructors themselves, each approaching the process in a slightly different way. The two major gifts that exert an influence on instruction style are Teaching and Exhortation.

The author of two New Testament books was Luke, the physician. In the first chapter of his gospel he wrote,

> *Several biographies of Christ have already been written using as their source material the reports circulating among us from the early disciples and other eyewitnesses. However, it occurred to me that it would be well to recheck all these accounts from first to last and after thorough investigation to pass this summary on to you, to reassure you of the truth of all you were taught* (Luke 1:1-4 TLB).

Luke is an example of someone with the gift of Teaching. A teacher does not have to be a member of a profession. He can be a thinker, a researcher, or a housewife— anyone who wants things to "make sense," for himself and others. Those with the gift of Teaching are especially effective in working with those at lower motivational levels because they communicate specific instructions and expectations, then follow up with close supervision and attention to detail. They try to make their students feel like individuals, free to progress at their own pace. Their content is reliable because they test information by scriptural principles instead of pragmatism.

When they are at lower motivational levels themselves, those with the gift of Teaching can be careless, disorganized, and anxious. Their students may find them haughty, sarcastic, and unduly critical. In some cases the misguided teacher tries to assemble a personal clique of followers.

Exhortation Style of Instruction

Look again at the passage from Luke chapter one. Luke possessed both instructional gifts, Teaching and Exhortation. Luke does not communicate simply a string of facts, but combines the history into a compelling document.

While the gift of Teaching is like planting seeds, the gift of Exhortation (or encouragement) is like watering those seeds. The teacher explains and the exhorter persuades. The teacher equips people on Levels 1 and 2. The exhorter helps them progress to Levels 3 and 4, forcing them to depend on God rather than on themselves. An exhorter helps them to persevere when they lose heart and keeps reminding them of the prize of the high calling of God.

The person with the gift of Exhortation can visualize organizational and spiritual goals and motivate people to work toward them. Exhorters provide an inspiring example, treating people as individuals as they build harmony and unity, even among a large group of people.

When exhorters become more interested in themselves than in promoting spiritual growth in others, however, their encouragement grows trite and their discernment faulty. As they forsake the Scriptures as their source of truth, they rely instead on worldly pragmatic considerations. Their enthusiasm fades into apathy without the Lord as the source of strength.

Getting Results through Leadership

Many families are together today because someone in the family had the gift of Leadership. Because of that gift, families have been able to withstand tragedy, survive the loss of a home, or recover from financial hardship. These families have begun small businesses and opened their homes to the handicapped and underprivileged. God said, "My people perish without a vision" (Prov. 29:18). Vision accompanies leadership.

Those with a gift of Leadership get results because they are prayer warriors and self-starters. Since they are confident of the truths of Scripture, they are oblivious to the taunts of others. They remain loyal and are able to spot the gift of Leadership in others and delegate responsibility to them. When they find a problem, they attack it creatively and plan a solution with great care.

When leaders become too conscious of their accomplishments, their self-confidence becomes arrogance. Ceasing to seek God's guidance, they interpret all questions put to them as criticism and insubordination. They become threatened by others' skills and abilities and begin to question their motives, refusing to delegate responsibility to them.

The family, church, or organization encumbered by this kind of leader is no longer a body at all but merely a mass of uncoordinated members. It is like a beehive where the queen retains her rank by killing all the queen larvae as soon as they are hatched.

Several years ago, a successful organization with close ties to government lost its administrator to a larger organization. To establish continuity, the company hired as a replacement a man who had previously provided governmental oversight to the company. Although he had been well liked in his former role, once he became the new administrator, he changed drastically. He began to exert total control, making all decisions himself and humiliating those around him who exercised any initiative.

The staff was unprepared for this change. Previously an outstanding staff known for its maturity and ability to operate independently, members were now treated as though they needed constant monitoring. Their freedom to make decisions was totally abolished. Some were forced out of their positions, and others left voluntarily. Within two years, the organization was in shambles, and the administrator was fired. What went wrong?

When the administrator first took the position, he realized that he lacked the technical skills possessed by the previous administrator and was even outclassed by the staff. This made him feel threatened, and as a result, his motivational level dropped. His jungle-survival response was to put down the people around him, something that only made his lack of skills more evident. This "queen bee" was doomed to fail.

Had the administrator's pride not been so strong, he could have depended on his staff to help him develop the more technical skills. Instead, he chose to get the staff before they got him.

Getting Results through Service

Just as those with the gift of Leadership are needed for getting results in the body of Christ, so are those with the gift of Service. These people take great joy in serving, often volunteering to work so that others may be free to do different tasks. They are flexible, sensitive, and generous with their time and material resources.

A church blessed with members who have the gift of Service becomes known as one of the most caring churches around. However, when people with the gift of Service rely on their own strength or begin to think they have not received proper acknowledgment for their services, they may decide that people are taking advantage of them. When self-pity sets in, they will withdraw and resist giving assistance, focusing more on serving self than serving others. After a while, they lose all sensitivity to the needs of others and help only when it requires no sacrifice on their part.

Bob was a church elder who had lost the spiritual perspective on his gift of Service. When someone asked his help, he would say, "I'll probably get behind in my work, but I'll see what I can do. I sure know how it feels not to have anyone help you when you need it. It happens to me all the time." Before long, anyone who had been helped by Bob found excuses to avoid calling on him. According to his words, this should have made him happier because he wasn't being bothered; instead he was devastated because he had suppressed his inborn need to serve. He had become like the biblical Martha who was so busy working and complaining that she never realized the significance of Jesus' presence.

Signs of the Gifts in Children

Children with the gift of Giving tend to be leaders who are vibrant, full of fun, and positive in nature. You will often find them engaged in games with other children. They demonstrate their appreciation openly. Because they are willing to share, other children sometimes take advantage of them. By the time they are older, they have learned by experience to be careful in their giving.

Children with the gift of Prophecy like to be around other people and they enjoy activity. As a rule, they are far more interested in realistic play than in "pretend" play. Because they see things as black and white, it is sometimes difficult to get along with them, particularly if they are highly verbal, as most of them are. They may be very hard on themselves and even reach a point of despair when they don't feel they have measured up to their own standards. Among friends their own age, children with the gift of Prophecy are often influential leaders.

Children with the gift of Mercy are the ones who bring home every stray dog or cat in town. They tend to be extremely tender and sensitive. Harsh words or tension in the home move them to tears. Because of their gentleness they often become followers rather than leaders. This quality gives them the appearance of being pushovers for the more aggressive children. However, if a bully violates someone's rights, the formerly mild, shy child will become like a tiger protecting her young. If necessary, this child will even resort to physical violence.

Children with the gift of Teaching often spend a great deal of time alone, reading or doing school assignments. They find it hard to feign interest in a school subject, preferring to ignore the work and get a poor grade. Children with a gift of Teaching seem strongly individualistic because they do not consider themselves bound by artificial controls. Their personal self-fulfillment is found not in the approval of others but in searching out facts and finding the truth.

Children with the gift of Exhortation are people-centered and are often dynamic speakers. Martin Luther King, Jr., for example, could stir audiences from the time he was a teenager. Children with this gift also love to tease. On the surface they seem to have a Pollyanna attitude, but underneath they are quite serious-minded. You can always depend on exhorters to simplify work projects to make them easy. They have little interest in activities involving mechanics or math, but they are fascinated by ideas and concepts, particularly those involving people. They relate easily to people and go out of their way to make people happy. They are generally achievers who are fun-loving, industrious, and wholehearted in tasks they enjoy.

Children with the gift of Leadership are often popular with other children of all ages. They enjoy the company of their parents and other adults, especially when they can be involved in activities with them. Children with this gift want to be at the front of the line and will run for every office and join every club that seems even remotely interesting. They generally have a wide range of interests and will sometimes "rush in where angels fear to tread." They are well-organized and have a tendency to plan and act in a rather systematic way. Given their zeal, that is probably what keeps them alive until adulthood.

One day I saw a neighbor's son named David in the woods behind my house eyeing a big oak tree. "What are you thinking about, David," I asked him, "cutting down the tree?"

He looked at me for a moment and said, "Do you think I could build a fort in the crotch of that tree?"

I looked at the eleven-year-old and said bluntly, "David, it would take at least five other people to do that. Your chances of finding five people in this neighborhood are pretty slim since only two children live here, and both of them are so young their parents would never let them up that high."

He nodded dreamily and said, "It sure would be a neat fort." Knowing David, I somehow did not think I had heard the last of it.

About two weeks later, on a Saturday morning, I woke up to the sound of sawing, hammering, and excited voices. When I went out to look, I saw seventeen children in the woods scampering over a tremendous pile of wood. David was standing off to the side, telling groups of three or four children exactly what he wanted them to do. In his hand he held a plan he had sketched out for a tree fort, complete with the length of each piece of wood he would need. One group was doing the cutting, one was in charge of getting the material up the tree, and another group was doing the building.

I asked David, "Where did all these people come from?"

He said, "Oh, they're all in my class at school. I invited them over to help me build the fort, and then my mom is going to have a cookout and they can swim in the pool." It turned out they were also experienced. David had carefully selected for his construction crew friends who had worked with their fathers in various home building projects.

"Where did all this wood come from?" I asked.

"Oh, my dad got it for me from Mr. Swanson. He was tearing down his shed, and when I asked if we could have the wood, he said yes if we would move it off his property. My dad said we could borrow Mr. Townes's pickup to take it away."

By the end of the day, his elaborate fort was finished. It is amazing what those with the gift of Leadership can accomplish. Without them it would be difficult to build the body of Christ—many members with different functions, but unified in the work of God's kingdom.

You can usually depend on children with the gift of Service to either have a pet or be working on their parents to get one. Because they get great satisfaction out of putting things together with their hands, they may limit themselves to a small group of friends. Although they like to help others, they have very definite ideas about how they want to be approached.

On Saturday mornings, ten-year-old Ricky could be seen all over the neighborhood talking to people and helping them wash their cars, trim their lawns, or do any number of odd jobs. "How fortunate you are to have him," the neighbors would tell his parents. They would shake their heads in amazement because Ricky wouldn't do a thing at home.

When a co-worker named Ted heard about the problem, he offered to help. He recognized something in Ricky that he had seen in himself—the gift of Service. He told Ricky's father, "People like us with the gift of Service don't like being told what to do because we have fun thinking up our own ways to help. When we get instructions, we lose interest and get resentful because part of our satisfaction is in seeing what needs to be done ourselves. We get overwhelmed with too many complicated tasks, too. Ricky will give up if things look too challenging."

Ricky's father agreed to try. It was a relief to think that the problem might not be with Ricky but with his approach to him.

About a week later, he walked exuberantly into Ted's office and said, "I can't believe the change in Ricky. He's more helpful to us than he is to the neighbors, and he hasn't slacked off helping them. He seems so much happier."

Ted said with a laugh, "You've got to treat us with respect, or we won't serve."

The Source of Knowledge

The Bible says that *all* the treasures of wisdom and knowledge are hidden in Christ. Paul added, "I tell you this so that no one may deceive you by fine-sounding arguments" (Eph. 2:3,4 NIV). In recent years, many fine-sounding arguments have been advanced to explain the breakdown in the family and the rise of despair among our young people. Since most of the authors of these theories failed to consult Christ, however, they have made almost no improvement in our society.

You may think after reading this chapter and taking the appendix/packet test that we are taking a simplistic approach to troubled relationships. Human interaction is complex, but we believe that God wants families to unlock its mysteries. For too long Christians have relied on secular "experts" to analyze their children and prescribe solutions that leave out God and bypass the parents. The only way for families to regain their sovereign right to raise their children in the nurture and admonition of the Lord is for parents to understand what makes each family member different and how that fits into God's overall plan.

The survival of the Christian family is important to God. He wants each individual to realize that he has great worth and is much loved. He wants husbands and wives to use their spiritual gifts to build strong families.

The concepts in this chapter and those that follow have transformed families. They have given encouragement to weary parents and helped adults and children understand who they are and what they can become. As you read, we hope you will continually seek God for clarification and confirmation of the principles in this book. His Word is the only authoritative source of truth, and anything that disagrees with that Word will not stand.

In that spirit, we want to present you with another concept that may startle you—a seemingly upside-down marriage that works. See what you think of this one.

CHAPTER THREE

PERSONALITIES

Charles leaned over and turned on the light.

"What's wrong?" Jeanne asked, startled.

Sitting up in bed, Charles looked at her with a mixture of concern and amusement. "I'm sorry, but I keep thinking about something I saw at Joe and Mindy's tonight. They don't act anything like Skip and Maureen."

Jeanne groaned and slid down onto her pillow again. "Is that all?" she said. "How can that possibly be keeping you awake?"

Charles said, "It's just that Skip and Maureen don't fit the model of the 'ideal Christian couple' the way Joe and Mindy do, but they still seem happy."

Jeanne could see that she wouldn't get any sleep until this midnight revelation played its course, so she made an inward resolve to make the best of it. Pulling on her robe, she sat up and tried to look interested.

"Did you notice how Joe took charge?" Charles asked. "He was the perfect host, greeting everyone at the door and directing them to proper places. 'Give your coat to Mindy. Join the others in the family room. Help yourself to a snack. Relax and make yourself at home.'"

"Meanwhile, Mindy was the regular dutiful wife, smiling and taking coats, keeping snack bowls filled, and excusing herself to finish dinner."

Jeanne said, "O.K., so that is your 'ideal Christian couple'—wife submitted to husband who runs the show. They complemented each other as host and hostess, husband and submitted wife. So what's confusing you?"

"How do you explain Skip and Maureen?" Charles asked. "He teaches third-graders while she is a businesswoman. When they walked in the house, Skip carried a dish in one hand and the two-year-old in the other. Maureen told him where to put the food and took the children to the place where they were supposed to play."

Jeanne looked amused. "Now I see the problem," she said. "Here are two Christian couples. Both seem happy, but their roles are reversed. Joe seems to be the head of his house, but Maureen seems to be the head of hers. It just blows your understanding of Ephesians 5, doesn't it? What are you going to do about it?"

Charles turned off the light, fluffed his pillow, and said, "There's only one thing we can do. Invite them over and get to the bottom of it."

Jeanne laughed. "O.K., I'll set it up, but we better pray that you don't cause more problems than you solve by trying to probe into their personal lives."

The next weekend, Charles and Jeanne ordered pizzas and invited their friends over. They didn't want the typical regimen of potluck buffet and stilted conversation. They wanted to discover how these Christian couples had resolved their relationships with Scripture.

As soon as the pizzas were gone and the small talk hit a pause, Charles spilled out what was on his mind. There was a long silence. Then Joe began to chuckle, then Maureen, Mindy, and Skip, and pretty soon they were roaring. "What's so funny?" chorused Charles and Jeanne.

Making Peace with Personalities

After the gaiety had subsided, the couples gave the nonplussed Charles and Jeanne a lot more than they had bargained for. Married life for these couples had not always been a bed of roses. In fact, a few weeks earlier both had been wondering how long they could go on without some change in their family life. Mindy loved Joe and appreciated his leadership in the home, but she sometimes found his highly directive style relentless and stifling. Skip could see that obviously Maureen was a good organizer for their family but he continually felt guilty that he wasn't following the scriptural pattern. That was before both couples went on a weekend marriage retreat.

The retreat speaker described four basic personality types. He called people like Joe and Maureen "Rulers" because they found it natural to take charge. Their Ruler tendency wasn't a negative for a woman and a positive for a man. Nor did it deny the divine order for homes. It just resulted from the combination of spiritual gifts God had given them and experiences they had throughout life. Joe's directive style made him a successful manager and strong church leader. Maureen's organizational ability helped her coordinate work and family.

However, the speaker cautioned that Rulers needed to make a conscious effort to be sensitive to the feelings of others. Such personal concern came naturally to people like Mindy and Skip, whom he called "Servers," but Joe and Maureen had to work at it. "If you love others you must reach out to them," the speaker said. "God requires it of you. Remember, even if you can move mountains with your faith you are still nothing without love."

"When I heard that," Mindy said, "you can't imagine what a relief it was. I thought there was something terribly wrong with me because I could be so happy one minute and torn apart the next. Half the time Joe didn't even know he was hurting my feelings."

The speaker also gave Skip and Maureen permission to be themselves. Even though God said that the man is to be head of the wife, He didn't make all men directive leaders and all women delighted servants. Sometimes God gives men like Skip a natural inclination to serve and women like Maureen a natural inclination to be a leader. Skip didn't have to be embarrassed that he was a third-grade teacher while his wife was in business. It had nothing to do with his biblical role as spiritual head of the house. Maureen didn't have to leave the church and sign up for "women's lib." She could fit right in with the body of Christ.

With the speaker's help, Maureen began to see how there were times when she should set aside her inclinations to direct so that Skip could be the spiritual leader at home and, when necessary, the bottom-line decision-maker. Without the Lord, she might resent such submission as bondage. With His help, however, it became her true liberation.

It is clear in passages like Ephesians 5 that husbands and wives are to submit themselves *to one another*. That means accepting each other but still living within biblical guidelines for appropriate family roles.

The two couples were able to apply these truths to raising their children as well. They began to see that all family relationships could be improved once they understood and accepted one another's personality style.

When one parent finds it easier to get along with one child than another, for example, it is often a result of personality differences. In the Bible, there are examples of the strife caused when parents like Isaac and Rebecca favored Esau and Jacob, respectively, and Jacob favored Rachel's sons, Joseph and Benjamin.

Even parents who try to love all their children equally struggle with guilt feelings when they have greater compatibility with one child than another. Instead of avoiding those who antagonize them or feeling continually annoyed, the parent and child who clash should recognize their natural differences and make a deliberate effort to bless and enjoy one another. It will be a broadening experience for all.

A Biblical Perspective on Personalities

If you had the money and the inclination, you could go to any number of secular seminars and hear somewhat similar teachings on personality to what you will read here. However, there are important differences. For example, most of those seminars are for the business world and do not transfer well to families. Also, many seminars teach that personality types are inflexible entities: You can discover who you are and what other people have done to hurt you, but no one can change you, not even God. Understanding your personality is often presented as an end, not a means to an end. The seminar leader may suggest ideas on how people relate to one another, but the main intention is to teach you how to fulfill yourself, even if it means manipulation of other people or broken relationships with those close to you. You are the center of your universe and everyone else has to make room for you.

It may not be obvious at one of those seminars, but the hidden agenda is often the same as Satan's whispered message to Eve, "You can be a god." The Christian is not to get caught up in such humanistic and man-centered theories. As the Apostle Paul wrote, "See to it that no one takes you captive through hollow and deceptive philosophy, which depends on human tradition and the basic principles of this world rather than on Christ" (Col. 2:8 NIV).

The Christian's goal in studying personality types should not be greater self-centeredness but greater God-centeredness. We study personalities to see how intricately

God has made us and those around us. Our goals are to discover how to build good relationships and then disciple one another.

In the last chapter you learned that the functional gifts provide the framework around which the basic personality develops. Before you were born-again, those gifts provided a semi-latent structure for your basic personality. After you were born-again, they became empowered by the spirit of God. As you grow spiritually and increasingly abandon yourself to God, these gifts begin to develop and blossom. They yield fruit that is reflected in the fullness of your personality. When you reach a relatively high level of spiritual development, other gifts that were less dominant begin to show up as well. Ultimately, as you reach the fourth level of maturity, you will discover that all of God's gifts become so evident in your attitudes and behavior that neither your carnal nature nor your past experiences have power over you any longer. Instead of being bound by the past you are set free to live abundantly in the present (John 10:10).

Four Basic Personalities

In the fourth or fifth century before Christ, the Greek physician Hippocrates came up with an explanation for personality differences. He theorized that one or more bodily fluids, or "humors," predominated in each individual. Too much blood made a person sanguine, or lively, he said. Irascible people had an excess of yellow bile, or choler. Black bile was responsible for dark, melancholy personalities, and phlegm produced slow, easygoing tendencies.

These Hippocratic temperaments—sanguine, choleric, melancholic, and phlegmatic—were eventually found to have no medical validity, but even though researchers since Hippocrates have classified over 1,600 personality types, a fourfold classification of personality has remained useful.

The four basic personality types we identify here are adapted from the work of LaHaye, Merrill, and others, as well as our own research. The research findings used have high validity. (See appendix for verification studies.)

The names we have given the four basic personality styles are Ruler, Designer, Promoter, and Server.

Rulers tend to be assertive, directive, and somewhat unresponsive to personal needs. Promoters are also assertive and directive, but tend to be more sensitive to individuals. Servers tend to be highly responsive but do not naturally assert themselves. They like to maintain a stable environment by seeing to it that everyone feels good and likes each other. Designers also like to control their environment but they do it through attention to detail. They tend to be more assertive and less responsive than Servers. Their methods tend to be analytical.

While you read about the personality tendencies described below, keep in mind that a negative side of each personality will show up among those at lower levels of motivation, just as in the discussion of gifts in the preceding chapter. The more positive descriptions of personality types characterize those at higher levels.

If you think about it, Jesus assembled about Him a motley crew. James and John were so volatile He called them "Sons of Thunder." Matthew was a tax collector, one of the most hated persons in the land. Peter revealed moments of brilliance, when he saw the truth about Jesus as Messiah, and moments of failure, when he denied the Lord. Mary sat at Jesus' feet while Martha fretted about the housework. All these individuals had different personalities, but each one played an important part in God's work.

As you learn to use the four general categories of personality described here, be careful not to lock yourself or anyone else into any one type. God made each person unique, so no one will completely fit any man-made formula. God has the right to intervene at any time to make changes, and all individuals naturally become different as they pass through the motivational levels to maturity. Persons have a tendency to act in a particular way, not a destiny.

Gifts Typically Dominant in Each Personality

The following chart refers back to the functional gifts described in chapter two. It indicates which gifts are dominant for each personality type.

Ruler
Appraisal Perspective: Prophecy
Instructional Style: Exhortation
Results Method: Leadership

Designer
Appraisal Perspective: Prophecy
Instructional Style: Teaching
Results Method: Service

Promoter
Appraisal Perspective: Mercy
Instructional Style: Exhortation
Results Method: Leadership

Server
Appraisal Perspective: Mercy
Instructional Style: Teaching
Results Method: Service

How People Interact

Depending on their personality types, individuals tend to interact with one another as follows:

Ruler	Designer	Promoter	Server
Extroverted	Introverted	Extroverted	Introverted
Governs	Manages	Encourages	Maintains

Highly directive (tells) ----- Highly responsive (asks)

Task oriented ----- People oriented

Prefers making decisions ----- Lets others decide

Attends to details ----- Downplays details

Keeps everyone efficient ----- Keeps everyone happy

What It Means to be a Ruler

People who fall into the Ruler category consistently make plans and complete projects through sheer determination. They are often oblivious to the cost to others, so single-mindedly do they pursue their goals. They are practical and forceful, with strongly held opinions on the best way of doing things.

Rulers can be prone to temper flare-ups when people do not meet their expectations. They may bitterly criticize others and then hold a grudge. In spite of this, because of their adeptness at marshalling forces and their dogged perseverance, they can strongly motivate the workers in an organization. Eventually, however, unless they change their tactics, no one will be able to work with them. They make good "hired guns," but may be ineffective for long-term maintenance.

RULER
Extroverted
Task-oriented
Likes to take charge
Dominated by gifts of Prophecy,
Exhortation, and Leadership

AT WORST
Domineering
Opinionated
Impatient
Critical of those
   with gifts of Mercy,
Teaching, Service

AT BEST
Submitted to Christ
   and brethren
Admits imperfections
Decisive, efficient,
   enjoys challenge,
   refuses to quit
Visionary, able to
   inspire others

One example of a Ruler is a famous principal. Before he took over, the high school was reportedly a dead-end dungeon full of drug pushers and drop-outs. Armed with a baseball bat and bull horn, he chased away the pushers and restored law and order to the former jungle.

His Ruler personality is probably the only one that could have cleaned up the hallways and attitudes of a place like that. According to some reports, however, because of his abrasive style he was unable to maintain the upward rise of student achievement nor work effectively with several teachers. A noble effort became stalled when justice was not tempered with mercy.

Notice on the chart on page 51 how the functional gifts tend to dominate when the Ruler is at a lower motivational level and how the Ruler ignores the other gifts.

At Level 3, Rulers still demonstrate mainly the gifts of Prophecy, Leadership, and Exhortation, but they are beginning to search within themselves for touches of Teaching, Service, and Mercy. They accept the value of others who have those gifts and realize that there is a place in God's world for everyone. These Rulers consult God, search the Scriptures, and seek counsel from other people before taking immovable positions. They have learned to control their temper. They still fight delay, but they understand that sometimes it is necessary. In whatever projects they undertake, they are able to be successful without injuring others. (See chart on page 52.)

When the gift of Prophecy is dominant, a Ruler tends to be more directive. When Exhortation is dominant, he tends to be more responsive. Sometimes, even at lower motivational levels, a Ruler will have strong input from the gift of Mercy, Service, or Teaching. Each person is an individual.

In the early 1960s, Pat Robertson, who had the personal style of a Ruler, believed he had heard from God that he was to purchase a television station in Portsmouth,

Virginia. In obedience to God's leading, with only seventy dollars in his pocket and his wife and small children to support, he negotiated a purchase plan for a television station that, in his words, "had about enough broadcasting power to go across the street."

The ensuing years were not easy for him and his family. Often they seemed to live a hand-to-mouth existence. The ministry often seemed close to financial collapse. Yet he persevered because God had given him a vision. He stood firm in the face of criticism from family, friends, and well-meaning advisors.

Ultimately, his faithfulness to God's call and vision yielded a tremendous ministry that now stretches worldwide and includes a cable network, a university, and Operation Blessing, an outreach to the poor that helps victims of tragedy and disaster.

Everyone called to leadership will have to face adversity, so they must have the courage and vision to do what God has called them to do. Without question, a Ruler submitted to God can accomplish great exploits.

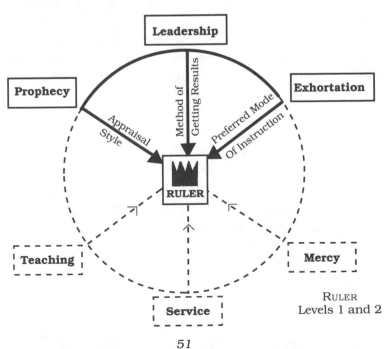

RULER
Levels 1 and 2

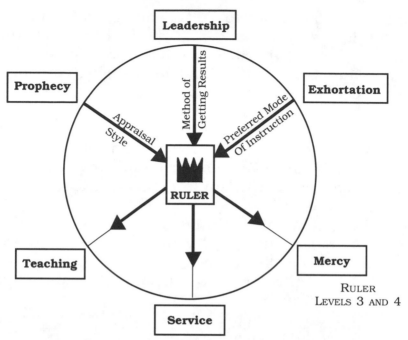

What It Means to be a Designer

Because Designers are sensitive to aesthetics, they create environments pleasing to the eye. Zealous workers, they are often perfectionists who excel at analytical tasks, establishing high standards for themselves and others. Not easily swayed from their course, they will persist even in the face of obstacles.

DESIGNER
Introverted
Task-oriented
Perfectionistic toward self and others
Cautious and orderly when leading
Pleased by attractive surroundings
Dominated by gifts of Prophecy,
Teaching, and Service

DESIGNER

AT WORST	AT BEST
Perfectionistic and self-critical	Aware only Christ is perfect
Cynical	Zealous
Susceptible to mood swings	Stable
Judgmental	Artistic
Overly punitive	Respected for self-sacrifice
Critical of those with gifts of Mercy, Exhortation, and Leadership	

Anyone who follows show-business personalities has seen more than once what results when a Designer without maturity is in a position of control. Consider the sensational singing stars who have an audience roaring to its feet and then go home and cry, have a few drinks, and inject numbing drugs to console themselves about their poor performance.

Look at the chart on page 54 to see the limited influence of the functional gifts on a lower level Designer.

As you can see from the other chart on page 54, at a higher level of maturity, Designers realize that those with the gifts of Mercy, Exhortation, and Leadership are important after all. They have more patience with those who have these gifts and seek them for themselves.

Some Designers have a dominant gift of Prophecy and therefore tend to be more directive. Since Teaching is dominant instead of Exhortation, they are more detail-oriented.

As parents, Designers tend to lead through control of the environment and details. They rely on established policies and procedures to help each child perform household chores.

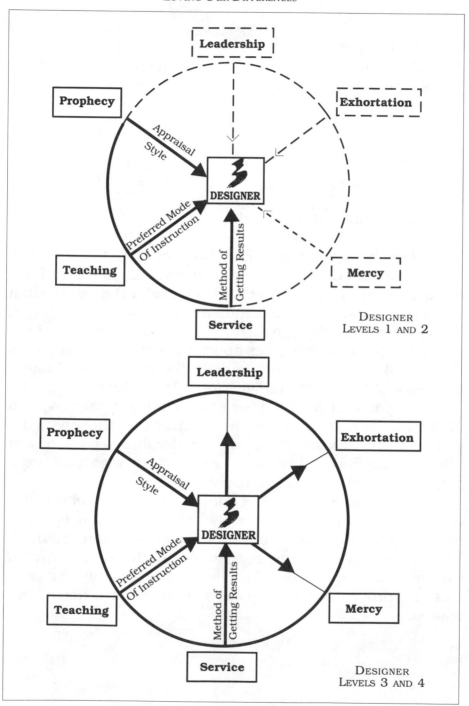

Leadership

Prophecy

Exhortation

Appraisal
Style

DESIGNER

Preferred Mode
Of Instruction

Method of
Getting Results

Teaching

Mercy

Service

DESIGNER
LEVELS 1 AND 2

Leadership

Prophecy

Exhortation

Appraisal
Style

DESIGNER

Preferred Mode
Of Instruction

Method of
Getting Results

Teaching

Mercy

Service

DESIGNER
LEVELS 3 AND 4

What It Means to be a Promoter

Promoters are known as "the life of the party" because of their genial wit, exuberance, and love for people. Their energy seems endless and they inspire others to action, optimistically predicting that everything will work out. Often highly compassionate, the Promoter is affected by others' needs and shares their feelings, crying and laughing with them.

Children of Promoter parents find it easy to relate to them. The Promoter is more likely to encourage and edify the child and not "put him down." Likewise, parents usually enjoy the company of Promoter children, who make them laugh with their imaginative style.

PROMOTER
Extroverted
People-oriented
Responsive
Dominated by gifts of Mercy,
Exhortation, and Leadership

AT WORST	AT BEST
Egocentric	Submitted to Lordship of
Wide mood swings	Christ
Disorganized	Attentive to others' needs
Prone to hasty	Disciplined
decisions	Dynamic in leadership
Critical of those	
with gifts	
of Prophecy, Teaching,	
Service	

Children who reveal Promoter traits are fun to have around but their bedrooms usually look like the Battle of Verdun took place there. Every corner of the house seems to

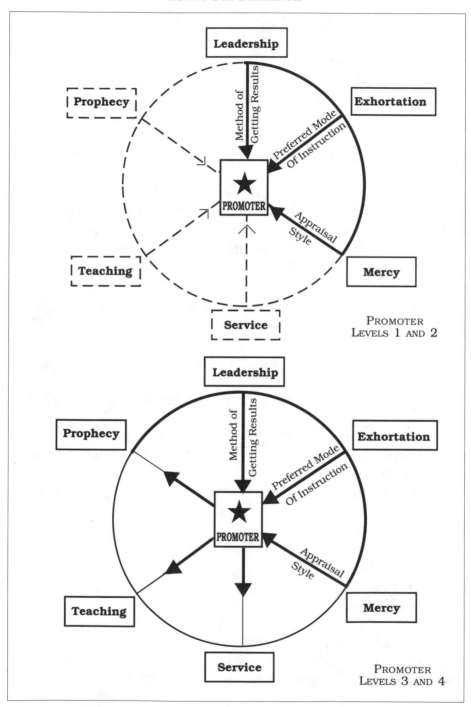

Leadership

Prophecy

Exhortation

Method of
Getting Results

Preferred Mode
Of Instruction

★
PROMOTER

Appraisal
Style

Teaching

Mercy

Service

PROMOTER
LEVELS 1 AND 2

Leadership

Prophecy

Exhortation

Method of
Getting Results

Preferred Mode
Of Instruction

★
PROMOTER

Appraisal
Style

Teaching

Mercy

Service

PROMOTER
LEVELS 3 AND 4

hold the remains of a different project left undone. If they are strongly egocentric, it doesn't wear well with the rest of the family, especially if they constantly boast that they can accomplish things that never come to pass.

Notice on the chart on page 56 how the functional gifts tend to dominate in Promoters at a lower motivational level, while they ignore the other gifts.

At higher levels of motivation, Promoters are beginning to search within themselves for Prophecy, Teaching, and Service and are reaching out to those who exhibit those gifts. (See chart on page 56.)

If Exhortation is their dominant gift, Promoters will be more directive. If Mercy is dominant, they will be more responsive.

In the opening story, Charles is an example of a Promoter. The relationship between his friends was important to him. When they were sharing a meal, he could hardly wait until the formalities were over before blurting out his questions. When he heard how much the retreat speaker had helped the two couples, he was moved to tears. There is no more loyal friend than a Promoter.

What It Means to be a Server

Servers are calm and dependable and never seem to get excited about anything. Because Servers are dependable, their spouses and children are extremely loyal. Often they are appreciated for their dry humor, usually offered as an aside because they prefer a spectator role to that of a participant. (See chart on page 59.)

> **SERVER**
> Introverted
> People-oriented
> Likes to help out
> Dominated by gifts of Mercy,
> Teaching, and Service

SERVER

AT WORST	AT BEST
Stressed by change	Trusting God's
Procrastinating	faithfulness
Unable to rule children	Seeking God's
Manipulated by loss	guidance
of love	Excellent parent
Critical of those with gifts	Servant leader
of Prophecy, Exhortation,	
Leadership	

No one was a more dedicated mother than Julianna. She stayed home with her children all the time they were growing up and was available to everyone in the neighborhood to bandage a scraped knee or give a hug and a kiss. Unfortunately, she loved her children so much that she could not bear to correct them. When they became disrespectful, she was stunned. Before long, her husband hated to go home at night because of the disarray in his home. Like his wife, he was a Server and couldn't understand why the children didn't respond to simple love. He became so frustrated that he resorted to shouting at the children when they misbehaved, threatening punishment that he never carried out.

Finally, they learned about their Server personality styles and were able to see how they were being manipulated by their children. Eventually, with the help of God, they were able to restore order and mutual love to their home.

When the gift of Teaching is dominant, Servers are more directive. When the gift of Mercy is dominant, Servers are more sensitive to details and technicalities and more responsive to the heartfelt needs of others.

Skip and Mindy in the opening story were both Servers. Mindy had a stronger gift of Mercy. She served and met physical needs, but she was more interested in being responsive to emotional needs. During the dinner at her

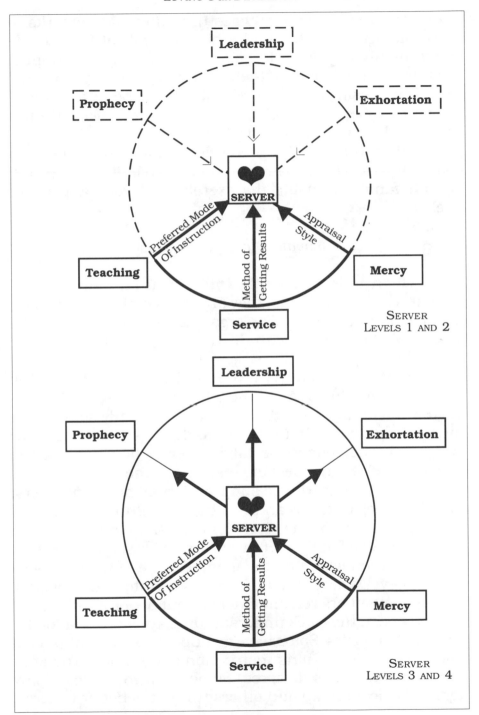

SERVER
LEVELS 1 AND 2

SERVER
LEVELS 3 AND 4

home, she would frequently gesture and make remarks to affirm her guests. Skip had a stronger gift of Service. He cared mainly for his children's physical needs—buttoning their coats and fastening their seat belts. His most natural way of expressing love for his family was by being a "behind-the-scenes" Server. His gift of Service made him an effective third-grade teacher. (See chart on page 59.)

When you have finished this chapter, you will have a chance to discover the basic personality style of each member of your family by using the exercises in your appendix/packet.

Loving Our Differences

When individuals reach full spiritual maturity and have access to all the gifts, they are still members of a body—whether family, church, or organization—and need to be surrounded by people with different gifts in order to make the body complete.

In our research we have found that in most healthy families all or almost all of the gifts will probably be represented. If a family needs Mercy, there is usually someone in the family gifted in that way. If Prophecy is needed for "law and order," someone else takes over. When none of the members exhibit the best expressions of the gifts, however, either from immaturity or suppression by other members, the result may be chaos and eventual dissolution of the unit.

If you look at the chart on page 61, you will see an illustration of a family, a church, group, or some other kind of organization where all the members are at a lower motivational level. There is some overlap and interaction of gifts, but most members remain independent of one another. For the most part, they lack understanding and appreciation for one another's gifts. Some have an opposite style of appraisal from others. Some think instruction should be carried out one way and others disagree. Some want to get results by aggressive leadership and others think it is better to serve.

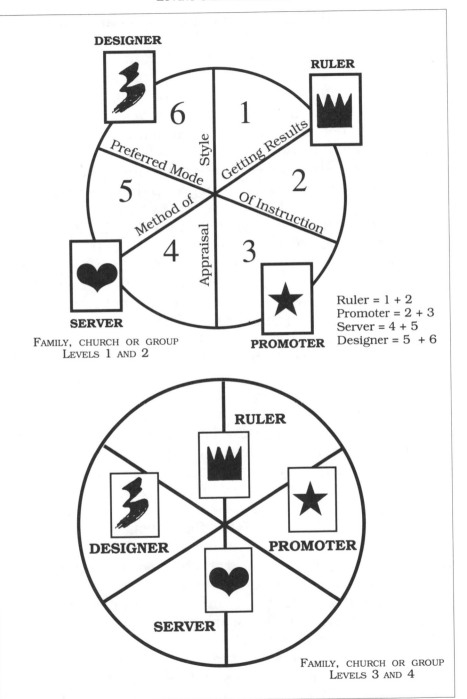

Ruler = 1 + 2
Promoter = 2 + 3
Server = 4 + 5
Designer = 5 + 6

FAMILY, CHURCH OR GROUP
LEVELS 1 AND 2

FAMILY, CHURCH OR GROUP
LEVELS 3 AND 4

There is general disagreement on mission and methods.

On page 61 is another illustration. This shows the impact of spiritual growth among the members. Because these members are at a higher motivational level, their roles and gifts are now interacting and complementing one another. Members realize they are dependent on one another but have not been required to relinquish their individuality. They are able to understand one another's viewpoint while still retaining their own personality and perspective. In short, it is a flourishing, colorful group that brings pleasure to the Father-heart of God.

If you feel tyrannized by a half-pint Ruler child who takes every ounce of your disciplinary strength, praise God that some day he may be serving God with such perseverance that no one can sway him from his course. If your Designer child drives you up a wall with her perfectionism and self-criticism, remember that some day she may be the one who rebuilds a troubled missions organization into a powerful force for world evangelism. When you are tempted to lock your Promoter in the bathroom and fumigate his bedroom, thank God he will some day be an encourager of the brethren, restoring those who have become discouraged to the joy and comfort of the Lord. And when your Server child never seems to do anything important in life but play quietly, consider that you may be growing a future mainstay of a caring church, someone who will reach out to the poor, the lonely, and the dispossessed.

If personalities are to be "Spirit led," reaching a high level of motivation through prayer and Bible study is essential. This applies to adults and children both. Understanding personality tendencies and growing within them will help you as a family member, an employee (or employer), and a church member. It will also help you find God's will for yourself and your children.

Even if none of you is ever a world-renowned personality, all of you can find God's purpose and walk in it. That is why it is important for you and others in your family to take the personality test in the appendix/packet. In the chapters to come, the principles you have just learned will be applied to the problems and opportunities of everyday life. Once you know who you are and who your family members are, you have important keys to self-esteem, teamwork in the home, relationships with teachers, and planning for careers. The next chapter deals with a skill that is essential to all family successes: the ability to communicate.

Chapter Four

Communication

Dad sat at his spot at the dinner table and absentmindedly watched the family troop to the table.

"Dad, I got my report card. Are you in a good mood?" asked fourteen-year-old Andrew.

"The car's making that noise again," his wife said between trips to the kitchen. "The last time that happened it cost us $400."

David, age twelve, quietly joined his older brother, and in the distance everyone heard Joey, age ten, chattering all the way in from his bedroom. "Hi, Dad. How's it goin'?" he said with a high five.

As five-year-old Elisabeth came running in she said

breathlessly, "Can I pray? Can I pray?" Oblivious to her request, Dad prayed above the rustling of chairs, "Father, thank you for your abundance. We ask that you bless this food and this time together. In Jesus' name. A . . ." Before the Amen was finished, Elisabeth said again, "Dad, let me pray!" After her five-second prayer, it was time to eat.

Dad reached for his fork. No fork. "Whose job is it to put out the forks?" he asked. Fingers pointed all around the table until Joey was identified as the culprit. "O.K. I'll get them," he said as he went to get utensils.

Between mouthfuls Andrew began reciting a long list of needs. "Dad, my gym shoes have holes in them. The rent on my instrument went up. I can't figure out my paper route bill. I don't have enough to . . ."

Joey, ignoring the fact that Andrew had the floor, blurted out, "Dad, do you know what my teacher said today?"

"Thanks for interrupting," Andrew snapped.

"You were being Mr. Motormouth again, weren't you?" Dad asked Joey teasingly.

"Dad, that's cold," David said with a smirk and everybody laughed.

Meanwhile, as Mom and Dad decided who had the floor, David began stuffing food in his mouth with his fingers like a B-movie barbarian. "David!" chorused his parents. Above the din Elisabeth raised her voice and her plate demanding, "Where's my food?"

By the time table conversation settled down and the children were speaking in turn, Dad was "off in space," planning how to solve tomorrow's problems at work. Mom, listening to the children's every word, glanced at Dad and wondered, "Doesn't he care about their needs?"

Individual Communication Styles

The scene at the dinner table represents the cross-currents of communication that constantly flow against one another in every family, regardless of its size. The conflicts may seem mild compared to the destructive behavior in many American families, but they demonstrate the subtle differences in individuals that can sow seeds of permanent discord if not dealt with at this level.

Communication means the way people speak, listen, and learn from one another. Most of us don't think much about our style of communication, but it is so important that the Apostle James wrote, "If anyone is never at fault in what he says, he is a perfect man" (James 3:2 NIV). However, most often we are greatly imperfect. James added:

> *The tongue also is a fire, a world of evil among the parts of the body. It corrupts the whole person, sets the whole course of his life on fire, and is itself set on fire by hell. . . No man can tame the tongue. It is a restless evil, full of deadly poison. With the tongue we praise our Lord and Father, and with it we curse men, who have been made in God's likeness. Out of the same mouth come praise and cursing. My brothers, this should not be* (James 3:6,8-10 NIV).

God gave mankind the ability to communicate so we could bless God and man, not curse them. The keys to communication that blesses the hearer are the same two commandments that Jesus summarized from the Law: love God and love your neighbor. Families would not suffer the strife and disintegration so common today if they practiced those commandments. We believe a great deal of reconciliation could occur if people were told how to understand the different styles of communication at work in their family or group.

Let's return to the dinner table and analyze the personality types represented:

Andrew, with his underlying gift of Leadership, was direct and forceful, reading off his list of problems to be solved and dominating the conversation. Elisabeth could be a Ruler, but she was still too young to show a consistent personality style. Dad had a strong gift of Leadership in addition to his typical Designer gift of Teaching. The Leadership gift gave Dad a more direct style of communicating. Mom and David with their Mercy gift had more of a responsive style. They were more sensitive to people's feelings. Joey was a Promoter with the gift of Exhortation.

Remember that God expects each of us to reach out and grow beyond the basic gifts that come naturally to us. For example, if a Ruler wants to be like Jesus, he must wash others' feet.

How We Send Messages

Each of us has a desire to communicate with others, to persuade them of our point of view. With a little knowledge of personalities and listening style, it is possible to get your message across quite effectively. The principle is this: Once you discover how the other person listens and learns, you alter your sending style to match his receiving style. In this section we will explain how to send messages effectively. The following section will deal with how people listen and learn, with descriptions adapted from the work of Merrill and Reed, in addition to our research.

Because powerful communication skills can be abused, the Christian needs to keep in mind certain general principles as he expands his persuasive abilities. These are the ethics of Christian communicators:

Have a motive of love. Your first step is to examine your motives. The only legitimate reason for a Christian to try to persuade another person is out of love. The Apostle Paul wrote, "If I speak with the tongues of men and of angels, but do not have love, I have become a noisy gong or a clanging cymbal" (1 Cor. 13:1 NASB). This applies whether you are speaking to a member of your family, to your pastor, to a friend, or to an enemy.

Be aware of God's will. Pray for those with whom you

desire to communicate. Ask God what He wants you to say.

Know God's Word. Make a habit of filling your mind and heart with God's words so that your own words will be pleasing to Him. Jesus said,

> *The good man brings good things out of the good stored up in his heart, and the evil man brings evil things out of the evil stored up in his heart. For out of the overflow of his heart his mouth speaks (Luke 6:45 NIV).*

Be a good listener. You can't respond to someone properly until you know what he has said. James said we should listen more than we speak: "Let every one be quick to hear, slow to speak and slow to anger; for the anger of man does not achieve the righteousness of God" (James 1:19-20 NASB). Careful listening is a major step toward esteeming others more highly than ourselves, of putting our opinions and needs aside long enough to actively attend to someone else.

Know yourself and your situation. As you learn to understand your own personality style, you will see how you tend to communicate with others. Be on guard against slipping into low levels of motivation. The higher your level, the more naturally flexible and accommodating you will become.

You may wonder, "Am I supposed to constantly change my style to match the listener like some kind of chameleon?" The answer is, not necessarily. The following guidelines will help you decide when and how to adapt your natural communication style for greatest effectiveness.

Casual, relaxed conversation. In normal settings, your communication style may be your own. As long as you can tell from the flow of conversation that there are no signs of tension or confrontation, be yourself.

Confrontation and conflict. When you sense trouble arising, modify your style to match that of the other party.

This is especially important when the other party is operating at a lower level of motivation. Because he will not be flexible in his communication, you must be the one to adapt.

Instructing a child. If you expect to teach your child anything, you will have to adapt yourself to his level of motivation. Children may remain at the same low level for years and parents just have to adjust to them. If one parent finds it difficult to change style, the other parent may be more successful in the teaching role. In the opening story, for example, Mom remained attentive even when Dad was off in his own thoughts. If you are a single parent, you will find help on this subject in chapter five.

The following list shows what communication characteristics appear as individuals in each personality group try to send out messages.

RULER: DRIVING COMMUNICATION STYLE

- Gets to the point. Is direct and precise and refuses to "waste time" by being wordy.
- Is often outspoken and assertive in stating opinions.
- Employs effective nonverbal communication (e.g., looks at his watch when he considers the conversation over).
- Maintains direct eye contact to make sure others are paying attention.
- Directs content toward results (e.g., "How many spelling words are on your list this week?" "When will you be finished washing the windows?" "How much did you spend at the store today?")

At lower levels of motivation, the Ruler is too direct and forceful to suit most listeners. At higher levels he adjusts his sending style to get the point across effectively without offending the listener.

DESIGNER: ANALYTICAL COMMUNICATION STYLE

- States things accurately and logically.
- Is often unaware of his own nonverbal communication

(e.g., may slump when speaking and employ little eye contact, even closing his eyes at times).

- Takes time to express his thoughts, making sure he is systematic and thorough.
- Analyzes situations (e.g., "He acted that way for the following reasons . . .").
- Often includes concepts, standards, and principles in what he says (e.g., "If he had followed the rules, this wouldn't have happened").

At low levels of motivation, the Designer will speak critically of himself and others. Like a low level Ruler, what he says often shows little regard for the feelings and real needs of the listener. At higher levels of motivation, the Designer will be more patient and helpful. Without casting aspersions, he will stick with the listener until he understands.

PROMOTER: EXPRESSIVE COMMUNICATION STYLE

- Is talkative and sociable.
- Speaks persuasively and articulately.
- Tries to inspire and build agreement in group settings; speaks optimistically.
- Emphasizes points with body language (i.e., uses hands frequently and maintains eye contact).
- Discusses dreams and intuitions and his ideas about making life better for people.

The Promoter at lower levels will focus talk on himself. If he interprets others' messages as threatening, he may retaliate with sarcasm. At higher levels, he will determine others' needs and then try to motivate them to meet those needs.

SERVER: AMIABLE, CARING COMMUNICATION STYLE

- Uses easy, relaxed tone of voice.
- Takes time to state his positions and decisions; is both reflective and wordy.

- Discusses feelings and relationships (e.g., "I know he had to do it but it must have hurt").
- Counsels others and makes them feel part of the team; seeks agreement before making decisions.
- Avoids eye contact in stressful conversations, such as discussing a problem with another person.

The Server at lower levels can be easily hurt by words. To protect himself he often avoids the person or topic. At higher levels of motivation he will ask leading questions, helping the listener to draw his own conclusions. When the Server does give advice, he is highly responsive to the listener's needs.

Listening and Learning

Now that you know something about how people send messages, you need to know how they receive them. As educator Mortimer Adler wrote in his book *How to Speak, How to Listen*:

> Listening . . . is primarily an activity of the mind, not of the ear or the eye. The most prevalent mistake people make about listening . . . is to regard it as passively receiving rather than actively participating.

The following principles of good listening are adapted from the work of Adler and others. They will be followed with descriptions of how those in each personality type tend to listen when someone is speaking to them. If you have despaired of ever getting through to your spouse or children, or of training your offspring to get the most out of church and school, this information is for you.

To understand the speaker's true message, you must stay alert. The good listener remains mentally active by constantly asking himself, "What is he trying to say? What is the actual message behind his words?" Since there is rarely an exact match between the motives, personality, and vocabulary of the parties engaged in a conversation, the listener must make an active effort to grasp concepts expressed in a variety of ways.

Listen carefully for the speaker's rationale for reaching his conclusions. If the listener "tunes out" during the presentation and hears only the concluding statement, he is likely to react inappropriately to the remarks.

Formulate questions in your mind as you listen. Keep alert by asking yourself questions like, "What will he say next? Why did he make that statement? I wonder if he will quote this verse . . ." Be careful not to draw conclusions too quickly, however. "He who answers before listening—that is his folly and his shame" (Prov. 18:13 NIV).

Take note of the speaker's nonverbal communications. Notice his use of eye contact, his posture, his facial expressions. "Is the speaker's posture closed, with little eye contact, or open and attentive to my responses?" The answers to those questions will help you interpret the tone as well as the content of the message.

Show respect by blocking out internal and external distractions. Active listening sometimes requires not only concentration but also planning ahead. For example, if you know your young children will be sitting through a sermon, provide them with quiet activities to engage their attention.

Jesus' statement "Do to others as you would have them do to you" (Luke 6:31 NIV) sums it up. When someone is speaking, pay attention. Don't sit with a blank expression or look as if you are ready to charge in and interrupt.

Good listening is a matter of the heart, mind, and will. It is also a matter of the body, since posture and eye contact communicate to the speaker that you are paying attention. Good listening is accomplished best at higher levels of motivation. Jesus said, "He who has ears, let him hear."

The following descriptions of the various listening and learning styles for each personality will help you know how to address them. These descriptions will be followed with an explanation of how to adjust communication style to motivational level.

RULER

- Listens for integrity and truthfulness.
- Pays attention in short spurts and then responds.
- Prefers to control conversation.
- Wants facts quickly.
- Asks, "How can I use this?"

DESIGNER

- Is sidetracked with own thoughts.
- May still be concentrating on previous conversation or occurrence.
- Likes facts, concepts, and principles.
- Needs time to reflect on information.
- Asks, "Does it make sense?"

PROMOTER

- Actively participates with speaker.
- Wants to receive feedback that he is motivating and encouraging others.
- Likes to experiment with ideas.
- Will listen more attentively if the conversation contains human interest or humor.
- Asks, "What if. . .?"

SERVER

- Avoids topics that might cause a confrontation.
- Listens attentively to speaker.
- Is more willing to listen if he believes he will learn something.
- Reflects on information before applying it.
- Asks, "What does it mean to me?"

So far, we have mostly spoken of the use of communication in families, but these skills also apply in other settings. Here is an example of how improved communication can build harmony in a church.

The Board of Elders of the Pleasant Valley Community Church seemed to be reaching an impasse. The meeting had been dominated by Howard, a Ruler who was unhappy with any delay in the church expansion they had been planning for months.

The pastor listened carefully but added, "I think we should talk about the families affected by the factory shutdown. Some of them are in dire financial straits."

Howard said somewhat irritably, "Look at these facts. We already have two services with people packed in every corner. The Sunday school rooms are overcrowded. Parking is impossible. What else can we do?"

This was not the pastor's first run-in with Howard. He appreciated Howard's assertive style in getting things done at business meetings, but he knew he was no match for him in a head-to-head contest. A Server, Pastor tended to withdraw from the conflict rather than risk troubling the waters. To him, a peacemaker was an appeaser.

If each of those men had considered the other's style of communicating and adapted their styles, the discussion could have gone like this:

Howard: Pastor, we have nine hundred people attending every Sunday; a third of those are children. Our sanctuary seats three hundred, maximum, and we use three trailers for Sunday school and children's church. Even running two morning services, there is still not enough room for visitors, especially visitors with children. We need more room to meet the needs of the people in our church.

(Howard still presented the facts, but knowing the pastor's Server orientation, he softened his tone and added "people needs" to his analysis.)

Pastor: You're right about the facts, Howard. We do have an urgent situation. Here's some more information to consider. Twenty-five percent of the working people in this town have been laid off, with about thirty families in our church affected. They need money for mortgages, rent, and food, and we've been draining the benevolence fund to help them. If we hope to sustain these families over an extended period of time, it will cost us at least $7,500 a month for this need alone. How much money do you think we will need for your proposal to expand the church facility?

(The pastor knew Howard responded to facts, so he used them to demonstrate the needs of the people.)

Howard: $125,000.

Pastor: Can you come to the next meeting with a plan to meet both needs?

(The pastor knew it was important to speak to Howard about results.)

Howard: I'll do that, Pastor.

(Howard might have hesitated, but he knew that it was important to Pastor to have a plan to meet the needs of the unemployed.)

The outcome of this meeting would be positive because the men took into consideration their own communication style and identified the style of the other, adapting themselves in order to obtain positive results. Their motivation for changing styles was not to manipulate or control one another, but to resolve a conflict in love. They used the "dying seed" principle Jesus taught: "Unless a grain of wheat falls into the earth and dies, it remains by itself alone; but if it dies, it bears much fruit" (John 12:24 NASB).

People who insist on having their own way may win a few contests, but eventually there won't be anyone else left on the playing field. Self-centeredness never bears good fruit, but those who are willing to die to self bear much fruit. In communication, "dying to self" can be achieved by adjusting communication styles to others in order to maintain and build up right relationships.

Motivational Level and Communication Styles

It's essential in good communication to adjust to the listener's motivational level. Often we deal with the same people on a regular basis. We instruct our children daily. We chat regularly with spouse, friends, co-workers, and supervisors. All of these people have their differences. Therefore, it is important to identify the motivational level of your listener and adapt your sending style to him if he consistently maintains that level. In a sense, you have to temporarily take on a different personality style in order to match the maturity level of your listener. Here are the best approaches for each level:

LEVEL 1 LISTENER
Address with style of Ruler

Tell the Level 1 listener directly and simply what needs to be done and what positive or negative consequences will follow each behavior.

LEVEL 2 LISTENER
Address with style of Promoter

The Level 2 listener needs a personal, affirming communication style. He wants to know what is expected of him and also needs frequent encouragement and approval.

LEVEL 3 LISTENER
Address with style of Designer

Use comments that show you have given his opinion in the matter considerable thought. State your goals and plans clearly.

LEVEL 4 LISTENER
Address with style of Server

He needs supportive, nondirective messages showing your concern and willingness to respond to him as an individual. Remember that when people are at Level 4 they do not need much direction. Their best character traits are already being demonstrated. The Server style is helpful in this situation because it communicates support in a nondirective manner.

As a general rule, you can often help individuals relate

to you at higher levels of motivation if you address them as if they were one level above where they actually are. For example, in a non-stressful conversation with someone at Level 2 or higher, try a Designer style to encourage a more mature response.

Conflict Resolution

One of the most important uses for good communication skills is the resolution of conflict. If you have more than one child and/or a neighborhood full of children, that may be one of your biggest jobs. If you persevere, you will speed the process of your child's advancement through the motivational levels and provide him with a powerful tool for future success.

Conflict is a normal part of life. It is part of the process of finding out who we are and what we stand for. Our responses to conflict play a large part in the person we become.

The Bible is filled with stories about people in conflict. Our goal in this section is to help you teach your child the biblical principles of conflict resolution.

Although personalities differ in the type of conflicts they encounter and the methods they use to resolve them, there are several common elements in any successful encounter:

- Time out to consider the problem
- Knowledge of how godly people handle conflict (from the Bible and personal experience)
- Love for enemies
- Prayer for guidance
- Reconciliation according to Matthew 18:15-20:
    a. Go to your brother alone (v. 15).
    b. If the situation is not resolved, take one or two witnesses (v. 16). (This could mean that one parent would bring in the other one to also confront the child.)

c. If still not resolved, bring it before an authoritative church group (v. 17). (The family might arrange for church counseling.)

d. Throughout the process, two or more should be in prayerful agreement (v. 18-20).

e. Maintain a spirit of constant forgiveness (v. 21-22).

The lower a person's level of motivation, the less patient and sensitive he will be in communicating to others. Even when adults progress to the highest level of motivation in some areas of their lives, they sometimes regress under stress. The following descriptions show how people of each motivational level and personality type typically get into trouble and how effective communication skills can help them get out.

RULER
LEVEL 1

Conflict tendencies: He tests limits, challenges illogical thinking or inefficient behavior (as he perceives it), says what he feels without thinking. For example, he may talk back when told it is bedtime or get angry when things don't turn out as he expected.

Resolution techniques: Set clear boundaries for his behavior. Suspend communication when those boundaries are crossed. This usually means a cooling-off period. Resume communication when the person is ready to be a more patient listener and a more temperate speaker.

LEVEL 2

Conflict tendencies: He may still communicate forcibly, demanding what he wants, but will sometimes squelch this urge out of fear of disapproval. He may state his displeasure with a decision but then suppress his anger and pout.

Resolution techniques: Urge him to explain the reasoning behind his requests or demands. Listen to what he says. Express approval when he speaks in an appropriate, constructive manner.

LEVEL 3

Conflict tendencies: Although more considerate of others' views, he may press the group to make a decision before all the information has been presented or all viewpoints expressed (e.g., where to spend the family vacation or which church to attend).

Resolution techniques: Affirm his ability to cut through emotions and get to the bottom line. Teach him about the different personality tendencies and communication styles. When he demonstrates flexibility in the future, show him respect and trust.

LEVEL 4

Conflict tendencies: He rarely engages in conflict, but when he does he may not realize it. This can happen when he communicates too forcefully with someone like a Level 2 Server or Designer who is easily hurt.

Resolution techniques: Explain the situation to him calmly, showing him the communication needs of people with various personalities at different levels. Point out situations where Jesus communicated differently depending on the receptivity of his listeners.

DESIGNER
LEVEL 1

Conflict tendencies: He may constantly complain and criticize (e.g., doesn't like the food, has too much homework).

Resolution techniques: Allow him to voice his opinions but not at the expense of others. Patiently and completely explain the rationale behind a decision. Suggest words he can use to express his needs without being critical of others.

LEVEL 2

Conflict tendencies: If his expectations of himself are not met, he may fall into self-condemnation. He may then try to control his environment by telling others what they are doing wrong and how it could be better (e.g., his sister's test was a B+ and not an A; the piece played on the piano had flaws).

Resolution techniques: Avoid criticism unless absolutely necessary. Speak aloud when you fail, modeling how you use coping statements or Scripture to keep you from getting down (e.g., "I'm fifteen minutes late for my appointment, but I'm not usually late; I'll do better next time with the Lord's help"). Speak positively about the person's talents and gifts outside of the conflict situation.

LEVEL 3

Conflict tendencies: He may hold on to a rule or principle too long, even to the point of being uncompromising (e.g., may not allow a family member to use his bicycle because it is against his principle of no lending).

Resolution techniques: Demonstrate a willingness to work out a solution acceptable to both parties. Point out other principles or rules that may take precedence in a situation (e.g., "Do unto others . . ."). Designers are systematic and normally reasonable. If you can demonstrate that their position was too restricting, without devaluing them as a person, they will be likely to see your point and cooperate.

LEVEL 4

Conflict tendencies: May hold to a plan even when it proves unproductive or impractical (e.g., using complicated rules and procedures to decide who chooses the TV programs).

Resolution techniques: Be rational and logical in explaining the impracticality of his plan or solution to a problem. Discuss the points that have merit and come to an agreement on a modified plan. Acknowledge his ability to plan and problem solve. Review Scriptures concerning man's ability to plan but God's power to bring it to pass. Explain that sometimes the best solution is the simplest.

Promoter
Level 1

Conflict tendencies: He may gossip, use sarcasm and ridicule, display emotional outbursts, and fabricate the truth. He may put down a person he doesn't like or make up a story about him.

Resolution techniques: Reaffirm your love for him but set strict rules forbidding gossip and lying. Allow him to express his emotions in a controlled setting.

Level 2

Conflict tendencies: He will say whatever comes into his mind, especially to gain attention (e.g., "Mom! Look at the fat lady at the door!"). He may keep arguing until proven right, as in a dispute over game rules.

Resolution techniques: Use verbal and non-verbal cues to let him know he is saying something inappropriate. Model for him a more tactful way to speak. Teach him to stop talking once his points are made in a discussion and then seek the decision of an authority.

Level 3

Conflict tendencies: Since he prefers not to lose the respect of a group, he may avoid open confrontation. He may even avoid resolving a situation in private or withdraw when he disagrees with a decision that seemed unfair or inconsistent (such as a ruling by a parent or teacher).

Resolution techniques: Praise him for his enthusiasm and skill in resolving other people's problems. Help him to consider other viewpoints. Explain the biblical model of confrontation in Matthew 18 (discussed earlier).

LEVEL 4

Conflict tendencies: Even at Level 4 he may still have difficulty admitting he made a mistake (e.g., making an agreement with someone to take an action that he knew was not the best thing to do).

Resolution techniques: Reinforce the fact that admitting mistakes is a sign of maturity. Review King David's life and the admonition in 1 John to ask for forgiveness.

SERVER
LEVEL 1

Conflict tendencies: He reacts against change, denies his faults, and may hold a grudge (e.g., may cry or be defiant with a new babysitter or teacher).

Resolution techniques: Take time to share and listen to related thoughts and feelings about hurts and disappointments. Let him know that you understand how he feels. Explain and model ways to collect facts about a situation and to gently confront. Try to explain your point of view or that of another person involved.

LEVEL 2

Conflict tendencies: At the slightest change of tone or sign of disapproval, he may feel hurt and timid. He will try to avoid eye contact and may not willingly confront the issue at hand.

Resolution techniques: In verbal and non-verbal ways, emphasize acceptance of him as a person. If you do disagree with him, be sure to make it clear that you love him even if you do not like some things that he says. Be specific about the issues you disagree on but try to resolve them in a tension-free environment as much as possible.

LEVEL 3

Conflict tendencies: The Server is least naturally equipped to handle confrontation and dispute. At Level 3, he may accept a solution with which he does not agree to avoid losing favor with a group. For example, he may go to an R-rated movie because everyone else wants to go.

Resolution techniques: Encourage his attempts to speak his mind in conflict situations, even if he is not as firm or articulate as you would prefer. Avoid quick judgments of his opinions until he has had ample time to express himself. Encourage him to go to others for prayer and support when the peer group is making decisions he doesn't think are right. Use Scriptures referring to persecution for righteousness sake.

LEVEL 4

Conflict tendencies: He may choose activities that are productive but prohibit him from getting the results that he should (e.g., his grades may start to slip due to too many church and school-related social activities).

Resolution techniques: Affirm his ability to listen to people and care about them. Discuss setting goals and being direct with people who ask him to serve at a function or club. Teach him time management skills that can be used when he is trapped in a group situation and needs to get on to something else. Discuss ways to politely get off the phone when it interferes with study time.

Building Family Unity

Jerry, a Promoter, was learning how to mow the lawn while his brother Paul, a Ruler, showed him how to operate the mower. Every time Jerry missed a spot Paul would get increasingly upset with him. The constant criticism made Jerry feel like a failure and caused him to do an even worse job on the lawn. Finally, Paul rudely relieved Jerry of his duties and completed the job himself.

The next time out, Bobby, a Server, was Jerry's teacher. Bobby made sure Jerry knew all the major points and then walked by his side as Jerry tried to mow. When

Jerry missed a spot, Bobby put his hand on his shoulder and explained what he had done wrong. Eventually, Jerry got the point and finished the lawn successfully.

At the dining table later, the boys' father talked about the incident. Without condemning any of them, he explained how their different personalities had affected their actions. He had explained the basic communication styles beforehand, and even ten-year-old Jerry had understood. After they talked about it, they saw that Bobby's way of communicating with Jerry produced better fruit. After that, the boys felt free to discuss all their communication problems, whether at home, school, or church, and quickly arrived at solutions.

Eventually Paul, the rude one, became more sensitive and patient when communicating with others. Of course, he needed approval as he began to demonstrate more mature communication skills. This is true of most people as their behavior changes from Level 1 to a higher level. The parents' patience and encouragement were crucial to Paul's growth and that of the other boys.

We recommend as an exercise for this chapter that you spend time with your children explaining these communication concepts, then take advantage of opportunities that arise to reinforce the teaching. The appendix/packet contains a family communication game to help everyone understand one another's differences.

Family unity is an achievable goal. It is something all parents should pray for. Jesus prayed, "May they be brought to complete unity to let the world know that you sent me and have loved them, even as you have loved me" (John 17:23 NIV). With good communication, a family that knows the Lord can come closer to fulfilling that vision and showing the neighborhood and the world the love of God.

CHAPTER FIVE

SINGLE PARENTING

"Statistics, statistics!" Lillian exclaimed.

Dee took her eyes off the road long enough to glance at her car-pool companion. "What's the matter?" she asked.

Lillian put down her newspaper. "Sometimes I get tired of reading about people like us in the newspaper, don't you? It says 'Thirteen million families are headed by divorced, separated, widowed and never-married persons. Four out of five are women. About 25 percent of the children in the United States live in families headed by single parents.'" She paused, folded the paper, and added, "Sometimes I still can't believe I fall into that category."

Dee's eyes were on the road but she said, "Jack passed away two years ago and you still feel it, don't you? At least you're a widow. In the eyes of the church that's respectable.

I'm divorced. That's a word that can invite disgust."

"I never found a church yet that offered me anything," Lillian said. "I'm not surprised they turned on you. I don't know how you've survived."

"I've survived because of Christ and because of support," Dee said.

"That's another problem," Lillian added, picking up her newspaper. "It says here that only 37 percent of single parents actually receive child support."

Dee laughed. "I don't mean that kind of support," she said. "I mean the body of Christ, people in the church."

"I thought they scorned you," Lillian said.

"That was in the beginning and at another church," Dee said. "Those people made me feel like Hester with a scarlet 'A.' I left there and tried another church, but they were just the opposite. They wanted to run my life. The pastor and elders acted as if I were totally incompetent to head a family. They didn't understand that I needed help, not a harness. I wanted someone to offer guidance and support but also recognize that I was the one who was accountable to Christ as head of my household."

Lillian responded, "My family tried moving in as soon as Jack died, but it didn't work. I know my children better than anyone. We had our own certain schedules and ways of getting along with each other. We needed to keep them so we would have some sense of continuity. They meant well, but they didn't realize that even though my husband was gone, I hadn't lost my mind. I had a good education and skills I could use." Then she said abruptly, "I'm curious. What did you finally find in a church that gave you the kind of support you needed?"

As Dee turned into the office parking lot, she said, "I found a church that practices the Bible where it says, 'Pure religion and undefiled before God and the Father is this: To visit the fatherless and widows in their affliction, and to keep himself unspotted from the world.'"

"This church saw me as someone who was afflicted

and offered to help instead of trying to take over. They realized that I wasn't just afflicted in a financial sense. I was afflicted by loneliness and doubt. I wanted to find another father in the church who could be my son's friend and role model, and I wanted to help choose who it would be. They were wonderful. Every time I called on them, they helped me. When I was too proud to ask, they asked me first. They never expected me to attend every church function because they knew how much time it took for me just to keep things running at home. Instead of criticizing me when I didn't show up, they made an effort to call and see how I was doing."

As the women opened the car doors, Lillian said wistfully, "I wish I could find that kind of support."

"It's done," said Dee. "I'm taking you to church on Sunday."

Catapulted into Single Parenthood

Dee and Lillian, as the statistics showed, are only two of the millions of single parents, both male and female, currently struggling to survive in America. Anyone may enter single parenthood through a crisis like one of these:

- Sudden death by accident or suicide
- Spouse's illness or depression
- Physical abuse
- Verbal abuse
- Constant quarreling and criticism
- Alcoholism
- Adultery
- Unwed pregnancy
- Abandonment
- Financial ruin

In cases of divorce, the husband and wife have often been unable to communicate for months or years. Since they never found anyone who could show them a solution, they gave up without discovering the power of God to bring spiritual and emotional maturity to any personality type and any relationship.

Many divorced persons and the surviving mates of suicide have problems with self-esteem. Often their children's character development has been neglected.

Some of these people have lost all hope in the power of God but, like a drowning person, reach out one last time to the church, hoping to at least find a friend. When a good Samaritan comes upon one of these people, he stops to offer help and takes them to a place of healing. However, although the church has a clear mandate to visit and comfort the afflicted, in cases of divorce it often acts more like the haughty priest in Jesus' parable than the loving stranger.

In this chapter, our goal is the restoration of single parents to wholeness and to their rightful place in the church. We will suggest a few skills that will help them make a new life for themselves and their families. We also want to suggest ways that the church can help single parents find a place of healing, regardless of the cause of their predicament. If the church is willing to follow the biblical model, it can use the single parenthood crisis to help its own people and also save the stranger in the ditch— people like Lillian in the opening story— who are searching for salvation.

What It Is Like to Be a Single Parent

Single parenthood is entered through a gate of trauma, and those who pass through desperately hope to find green pastures on the other side. Instead, what they find is a rocky path full of obstacles. With the help of God and His church this pathway can be cleared, but first there must be an understanding of what feelings stand in the way.

This is how the newly single parent feels:

Grieving and remorseful. Regardless of the cause of the new status, every single parent has periods of sadness and self-criticism regarding the relationship that has ended.

Angry. The person may be furious at herself, her ex-mate, her parents, an adulterous liaison, the church, and even God.

Lonely. The single parent is not only without a spouse but also no longer welcome in gatherings of young couples.

Overwhelmed. She must single-handedly coordinate all the family bill-paying, discipline, chores, maintenance, trips to the orthodontist, baseball games, recitals, and everything else that young children find to do.

Financially troubled. Two out of three single parents have no child support payments to supplement their income. Fifty-five percent support their families on incomes under $20,000 per year. Most are women, many are unskilled, yet they are suddenly forced to pay for child care and every other household expense out of a meager paycheck.

Forsaken by the church. Many churches are oriented toward families and hostile to divorced people. Social gatherings may emphasize couples. Married people may be the only ones considered for leadership roles. Although they usually have some outreach to members who express a need, many churches neglect to offer help to those unable to ask for it.

Questioning God. All the "Why me?" questions that every single parent asks will be accentuated if the person is a member of an uncaring church. Eventually, the hurting person may reject God Himself.

How to Help

The most important goal the church can accomplish in discipling the single parent is to facilitate her return to a higher motivational level where she can experience Christ's power in her life. Stress tends to cause a drop in motivational level in all but the strongest believers. The long-term stress associated with death and divorce is especially damaging. In the single parent, especially one who has lost confidence in God, this drop in motivational level is evidenced by self-centeredness and bitterness. This may be complicated by other personality defects that caused the divorce in the first place. Thus the person most in need of help and restoration may be the most difficult to get along with.

Recall the Old Testament book of Ruth. When Naomi's husband and sons died she returned to her home and told her friends, "Don't call me Naomi. Call me Mara, because the Almighty has made my life very bitter. I went away full, but the Lord has brought me back empty. Why call me Naomi? The Lord has afflicted me; the Almighty has brought misfortune upon me" (Ruth 1:20-21 NIV).

Here are typical effects of the drop in motivation as it shows up in each personality type:

The *Ruler* drops to a level where she is impatient and critical. She takes charge of her family and church responsibilities in a domineering, unyielding manner.

The *Designer* becomes cautious and introverted, heaping self-criticism on herself. When her children leave the house in a mess it makes her extremely angry. She keeps her children on edge as she continually changes moods, punishing them harshly and erratically.

The *Promoter* single parent is terribly hurt because not only her spouse but also her friends seem to be abandoning her. Like a bird with a broken wing, she looks hopelessly at the world outside and is unable to enjoy it. Her home becomes chaotic with everything in disarray. She begins to make hasty, unwise decisions. She criticizes the pastor and church people whom she feels have let her down.

The *Server* finds it difficult to deal with any change, let alone something of this magnitude. As a single parent, she runs into difficulties as she begins to procrastinate in everything. She is so desperate for love that she withholds correction from her children and neglects their discipleship process.

None of these changes is irreversible. The change

came in Naomi when she experienced the love of her daughter-in-law and the support of her relatives and friends. She saw God was at work after all and became joyful and grateful.

When the single parent begins to trust God again and receives love and support from family and church, her motivational level will rise. These will be the results:

Ruler. Once she recovers enough to return to a higher level of motivation, this single parent will take charge of her family in a positive way and persevere against every obstacle, telling them as often as they need to hear it, "We are going to make it."

Designer. Once she reaches the higher levels of motivation, the Designer will refuse to give in to frustrations, providing much needed stability for the family and earning her children's respect.

Promoter. At higher levels, the Promoter will overcome her backsliding, admit her weaknesses, and turn over her home and family to Christ. She will become a dynamic leader for her children, attentive to their personal needs.

Server. The Server at higher levels will recognize her failings and look to God for guidance and instruction. Her love and consistent discipleship will help the family work as a team and stay together. She will even be able to help the children forgive themselves and their parents.

Five Steps to Success

Let's look at steps the single parent can take to overcome problems and begin the rebuilding process to higher motivational levels. First we will discuss what the parent can do and then demonstrate the powerful role that the church can play in meeting needs and thus raising levels of motivation.

Single parents faced with seemingly insurmountable problems should use the following steps to discover the "way of escape" God has provided (1 Cor. 10:13):

STEPS TO SUCCESS FOR SINGLE PARENTS

1. *Define the problem and pray about it.* Be as objective as possible.
2. *Assess the family members involved* in the problem to determine their motivational levels, gifts, and personality styles.
3. *Determine qualifications needed in a helper.* Consider the ideal motivational level, gifts, and personality someone should have in order to fit in with your family's need.
4. *Consider possible helpers* Look around the neighborhood, church, and other groups to see who is familiar with your situation and might be the person to help you.
5. *Solicit help.* After prayer, ask for assistance from the person or persons who fit your qualifications. To be effective with your request, use the communication method best suited to his personality (see chapter four).

(In your appendix/packet you will find a Problem-Solver Worksheet for Single Parents.)

Define the Problem

Because of the highly emotional nature of problems faced by the single parent, it is important that she make an attempt to examine her situation objectively. Let's apply these principles to the story of Jessica.

Jessica greeted her mother at the door with the news, "I got kicked off the soccer team for missing practice yesterday." With tears in her eyes Jessica said, "You wouldn't take time off from your job to take me, and now I can't play any more."

Jessica's mother, Betty, was immediately stung with

guilt and anger. Unable to face her own inability to meet her daughter's needs, she reacted with anger toward the coach. "That's not fair!" she exclaimed. She thought, "That pompous fool! He doesn't care anything about my daughter. He just wants to act like a tyrant over that team."

When Betty took time later that night to pray about the problem, she realized, as she poured out her heart to the Lord, that she needed to go back and look at Jessica's problem again. Her initial reaction had been neither Christian nor productive.

She decided the best way to look at it objectively was to write it down, just as an outside observer might have seen it. Simply stated, her problem was as follows:

- The coach cut Jessica from the team because he thought she was irresponsible.
- Jessica needed a more dependable ride to practice.
- Betty would have to find someone else to drive her daughter to practice.
- Betty needed to explain the situation to the coach, assure him that she had arranged for a ride, and ask him to reconsider his action.

Assess the Family Members Involved

Once Betty had defined her problem, she took a look at the family's motivational levels, gifts, and personalities.

Jessica was a bubbly, excitable Promoter usually operating at Level 4. After school she liked to talk about what had happened to her all day before she was ready to concentrate on sports or anything else. Betty also was a Promoter and had the gift of Teaching.

Determine Qualifications of Possible Helpers

Betty's immediate need was for a ride to soccer practice, but she wanted to arrange more than transportation. She wanted someone who could befriend Jessica as well. The best personality style for this need, she decided, was a Server.

Consider Possible Helpers

Betty's next step was to pray and ask God for a Server who could take Jessica to practice. Some of the potential drivers she knew didn't fit her need for a Server, although she could ask their help if no one else came to mind. However, when she remembered another woman who worked at home and volunteered her time in the afternoon, she decided to contact her.

Betty also needed the help of the coach. She knew that he would be more receptive to her request for help if she approached him correctly. Since she had only met him once, she had to make some assumptions based on the way he handled practice. Since he tended to be extremely well organized and demanded that his players adhere to strict rules about attendance, she assumed he was a Ruler or Designer.

Solicit Help

Now that Betty knew what she had to do, she was tempted to do nothing. Suddenly she felt humiliated to be asking near-strangers for help. However, after more prayer she recalled the commandment to "serve one another in love" (Gal. 5:13 NIV). Unless others knew her needs, they would be unable to serve her. Instead of feeling humiliated, she saw it as an opportunity to trust God to use other people in her life.

Before she made her contacts, Betty prayed that she would have the right attitude and know the right words to say. She wanted to let others know that she accepted responsibility for the actions of herself and her daughter, but she was faced with some matters she simply could not handle alone.

When Betty called June, the woman who did volunteer

work, she first inquired about her family and busy schedule before asking for help. Since June was a Server, Betty used information on Jessica's emotional needs in the conversation as well as raising the problem of transportation. June responded quickly, "I'll be glad to do it," and would accept no money for expenses.

Betty's next task was a personal contact with the coach. At the next scheduled practice, she and Jessica arrived just as the team was coming together to start. Betty walked up to him and said, "I'm sorry that Jessica missed her last practice. I can certainly understand why you thought she was irresponsible and put her off the team. I take full responsibility." Because she knew he was a Designer or Ruler, she then gave him a factual description of her circumstances, without becoming emotional, and concluded with the solution she had devised with the help of June.

"I don't know," the coach said. "The other players might think I was being too soft on her." Betty carefully repeated the facts and her solution, affirming his position of authority, and asked him to reconsider. He consented.

It is true that single parents face more serious problems than arranging for a ride to soccer practice, but even small crises take on larger proportions when someone faces them alone. The point is that single parents do not have to be overwhelmed, nor do they have to do everything by themselves. They can make a deliberate choice to analyze their problems and make decisions, with the help of God, including the decision to involve other people.

Reaching Out to the Church

When a single parent attends a church that is supportive and helpful, that fellowship is the logical place for her to look for help.

Consider this example.

Dianne was a single parent with three sons, two of whom had personalities compatible with their mother, and the third, twelve-year-old Peter, who was always challenging her authority. After the divorce, Peter's motivational level dropped, and his grades declined. Feeling rejected by his father, he set unrealistic standards for himself. When he couldn't meet them, he became so anxious that he slipped even more. He became so critical of himself and others that he antagonized members of his family and lost all his friends.

Dianne took him to a counselor who, after several sessions, recommended that she find a man to befriend Peter. Dianne had no idea whom to ask, but she prayed, "Dear God, give me wisdom. I need someone Peter can look up to, who will love Peter and let himself be loved. Please send me one of your children. I can't do it alone."

After she prayed, Dianne felt a sense of peace. She decided her first step was to analyze her situation. She proceeded according to the five-step process, but this single mother reached out and asked her church for help.

Her basic problems were personality conflicts between herself and her son and the lack of a father figure in her son's life. Dianne, a Ruler, conflicted with her son, a Designer, especially since Peter's motivational level was dropping and he exhibited the less desirable traits of a Designer. Peter needed a compatible father figure who could fill the void in his life. It was important for him to have someone with whom he could successfully communicate and whom he could imitate. She decided that a Promoter would be the most likely person to show Peter encouragement and approval.

Dianne didn't know any men who could meet this need, so she enlisted the help of the pastor. After she described her problem to him, he gave her three suggestions, answering her questions related to the potential helpers' motivational levels and personalities. When he was unsure of anything, he called in his wife and together they were able to give her a good picture of each person.

As nearly as Dianne could tell, the three candidates were a Ruler, a Promoter, and a Server. All were functioning at least on Level 3. After prayer, Dianne decided to speak to Richard, the Promoter.

Dianne invited Richard and his wife for dessert and presented her need to them. They were warmly receptive and Richard promised to pray about it. Richard's commitment to Peter began with prayer. He knew if he rushed into a relationship and then found it wasn't God's will, Peter would have the devastating experience of losing another man from his life. He would be certain to blame himself.

If Richard had declined, Dianne would not have been lost. She could have gone back to prayer and repeated the five-step process. Because of the body of Christ, she would always have someone to help her.

The Church Reaches Out

Christians must not only be responders to those like Dianne who ask for help, they must also keep watch for those who are silently going under. Consider this example:

When William's wife died, he was left with two daughters, ages five and fourteen. His older daughter was fairly mature, but the younger one, Sarah, provoked her father daily as he tried to prepare her for kindergarten. By the time he arrived at work every day, he was emotionally distraught.

William's Sunday school teacher, Wayne, didn't have to be told that there were problems in the home. When he saw William and Sarah together at church, he recognized their Designer personality styles and realized they had dropped in motivational level since the tragedy. Both had become demanding and inflexible, and it was a volatile combination. As a result of his observations, Wayne offered to help William walk through the steps of the problem-solving process because he was too overwhelmed to see clearly what was wrong.

Once the problem was defined, personality qualities assessed, and an ideal helper envisioned, Wayne took the initiative to ask around at church to find who might be available to help out with Sarah before school. Mrs. Hess, a woman whose daughter also attended Sarah's school, seemed like a good candidate. She had a Server personality with strong gifts of Service and Leadership. She had the ability to be direct and to the point while meeting people's needs at the same time. Wayne also realized that Mrs. Hess usually operated at Level 2. As long as William expressed frequent approval of her efforts she would probably be motivated to continue helping.

When Wayne spoke to Mrs. Hess, he presented William's problem in terms of Sarah's emotional needs and the disruption of her relationship with her father. Instead of asking for a long-term commitment, something that would be overwhelming for a Level 2 Server, he asked her to help out for just one morning to see how it worked.

When Mrs. Hess arrived before school the next day to pick up Sarah, she was faced with an immediate problem. Sarah wanted to wear her expensive new shoes to school to show her friends, but William refused to let her ruin them on the playground. Sarah was crying and William was standing with his jaw set and his face red.

Mrs. Hess bustled in and took charge. "Sarah," she said, "let's put your new shoes in a bag. You can carry them to school and surprise your friends. Put them on while you're in the classroom and then change into your old shoes when it's time for recess." As she spoke, Mrs. Hess watched William to make sure he approved. As soon as Sarah heard Mrs. Hess's plan she visibly brightened. Running to the kitchen for a paper bag, she returned with her face wreathed in smiles.

Mrs. Hess had exercised her Leadership gift to take charge and end the stalemate. She used her Service gift to meet the needs of a little girl and her protective father. William told Wayne later, when he called to ask how it went, "I can see now that I don't have to play the tough guy all the time. When my wife was alive, she had a gentle touch like Mrs. Hess that I never appreciated. I told Mrs. Hess that she was filling an empty place in Sarah's life, and she looked terribly pleased. For the first time in weeks I actually went to work with a sense of peace."

Wayne made a special effort to call Mrs. Hess and repeat William's remarks. She was so pleased that she said, "I'm just doing what the good Lord wants. Tell him I'll come again tomorrow and keep coming as long as they need me."

When Single Parents Remarry

Many single parents never remarry and raise their children alone, but others find a new mate who conforms to biblical guidelines for remarriage.

In choosing a new spouse, single parents should consider all the characteristics of personality and motivational level that have been discussed earlier. Their goal should be to form a new relationship in Christ that will be a permanent bond for life.

Once the marriage has occurred, of course, there will still be problems to work out, but none of them is insurmountable. The most important step is deciding that no matter what happens, the couple will seek the help of God and His people to make this marriage work.

Here is an example of how one family worked through their period of adjustment using the skills taught in this book.

Sam was the successful manager of an assembly line when he met Suzette. A Designer with a strong gift of Teaching, he had been leading his Sunday school class in a disciplined search through the Scriptures. Suzette's outgoing personality and enthusiasm for his classes were attractive to him and he soon began spending time with this widow and her three children. To the excitement of everyone in the church, he eventually asked her to be his wife.

Although the children had welcomed their new father, a conflict developed that soon threatened their newfound happiness. When Suzette was a single parent working full time, she needed the constant cooperation of her children, ages eight, ten, and twelve, to keep up the household. They had advanced to motivational levels 2, 3, and even 4 as they took on this responsibility.

When Sam became the head of the house, he never took time to assess the motivational levels and personality styles of the children. He just assumed that, like some of his employees on the assembly line, they needed someone to tell them what to do. When eight-year-old Ziggy forgot to make his bed, Sam scolded him at the supper table that night. He told twelve-year-old Becky she would have to fix dinner for the next week when she was late for dinner because of an after-school cheerleading practice. And he warned ten-year-old Franky he couldn't play on the basketball team unless he did a better job mowing the lawn.

Sam realized when he moved in that there were informal policies in operation concerning household chores, but he was uncomfortable with the lack of definite procedures. He immediately set about establishing stringent standards with numerous checklists and requirements for his approval. Some of his changes had good results, but the general effect of his actions was demoralization and a general drop in motivational level of the children. When the children complained privately to their mother, she was reluctant to undermine his authority as head of the household.

Even without a direct confrontation from his wife, however, Sam realized he was in trouble. He sought out her brother, Tom, who had become a supportive friend. Over a game of golf Tom told him gently, "The children are angry with you because they say you came in and began treating them as if they didn't know anything about taking care of the house. Some of your suggestions were helpful, but without realizing it you took away too much control. They had grown up a lot since Terry died, but you were sending a message that they were childish time-wasters. They had been helping out because their mother said it was part of being on the family team, but you used chores as penalties. They don't want to try any more because you seem to think they're incompetent." After they prayed together, Sam expressed his appreciation for Tom's friendship and honesty.

When Sam got home, he called a family conference and apologized for not getting to know them before he began issuing orders. "The truth is," he told the children, "you do better work than some of the people at the plant. If we ever have a misunderstanding again, I want you to feel free to talk to me about it. We all need each other." In the days that followed, Sam changed his style to match their personalities and motivational levels and saw them blossom once again into maturity.

A Plea to the Church

We have included this chapter in the book in the hope that single and stepparents will see that no situation is impossible if they know the love of God and His people. We also hope that the church will gain a new understanding of its responsibility to include all single parents in its embrace.

In the past, many churches have been so appalled by the high divorce rate that they have considered it their duty to be harsh with divorced people lest others follow their example. They have not considered a divorced person to be in the category of widow or widower, because they saw divorce as one of the worst sins a person could commit. The church has also brought an extra load of grief on the survivors of suicide victims by claiming that such an action is an unforgivable sin that eliminates the person's chance to be saved.

Churches have also misunderstood their role in dealing with difficult divorced people. They saw a person whose unpleasant behavior contributed to the destruction of a family unit, someone whose personality characteristics were now even worse without the balancing input of a spouse, and they rejected that person instead of working to correct the behavior through discipleship.

These practices, whether through ignorance or design, have caused the church to abandon its proper role of restoration. Some divorced persons are innocent victims, but even if they are partly to blame, they need forgiveness and healing, not condemnation. Regardless of past sin, the church is to meet the needs of its repentant people whenever they are distressed or afflicted. One tool is the problem-solving worksheet for single parents in the appendix/packet.

The church has lacked understanding about how to help the single parent and, as a result, has either abandoned them or tried to control them. Some pastors or elders have usurped the role of head of the house instead of allowing the single parent to remain in charge. Pastors and elders can meet many needs, including finances and friendships with children, without interfering in the autonomy of the family structure. Their goal should be to "visit" the single parent in their affliction. That means allowing the single parent to train up her children in the way God tells her that each one should go.

When confronted with a person struggling to overcome negative character traits, the church should avoid judging and condemning these people and instead begin discipling them to higher levels of motivation. This process requires agape love, the kind that forgives seventy times seven and never gives up.

As you have read through the various stories, you should have seen a common thread throughout—the need for prayer. The single parent is totally dependent on God as a partner. As it says in Isaiah 54:5-7 (NIV): "For your Maker is your husband—the Lord Almighty is his name . . . The Lord will call you back as if you were a wife deserted and distressed in spirit—a wife who married young, only to be rejected . . .with deep compassion I will bring you back."

CHAPTER SIX

HOW TO GROW CHARACTER

"I love it! I love it!" exclaimed Gina, looking with glee at the test results spread across the kitchen table. "Now we know our children's motivational levels, functional gifts, and personality tendencies. We even know all about each other!"

Thad pushed away his coffee cup. "So what?" he said. "What do we do with all this information?"

Gina was startled. As a Designer, a stack of information on the table was all she needed to feel something had been accomplished. But Thad was a Ruler. He wanted to know the bottom line. "I'm sorry," he said, "but what are we going to do with these megatons of data?"

"I don't know," Gina said sheepishly, "but I think we'd better find out." It wasn't long before both of them had an unexpected answer.

Thad and Gina were the parents of three children, including an aggressive nine-year-old daughter. Every day with Sandra brought some new challenge to their peace of mind. They found that raising a family was never dull. Sometimes it was downright uncomfortable when they had to use the experiences of family life to mold their children's character.

Sandra had made a profession of faith in Christ, but like new believers of all ages she stumbled through growing stages of spiritual growth. These stages often parallel the levels of motivation discussed in chapter one. When she was born again, seeds of her future faith were sown, but circumstances would arise to threaten the growth of those seeds to maturity.

Sandra was blessed to have two loving parents—imperfect, to be sure, but people who loved God. They watched over that seed, feeding, watering, and cultivating it so God could give the increase.

About a week after Thad and Gina's discussion, Sandra found herself in big trouble. She arrived home from school proudly wearing a brightly colored jacket her parents had never seen before. "My friend gave it to me," she said. Gina and Thad were somewhat skeptical, so they asked a few questions. Before long, they discovered that Sandra had found the jacket on the school bus, left behind by a girl she did not know very well. Instead of trying to return it, she decided to keep it for herself.

Thad and Gina were shocked at their little girl's behavior. It seemed to be the opposite of everything they had tried to teach her. In order to successfully explain to Sandra all the issues at stake, Thad and Gina had to call to mind all they had been learning about her motivational level, gifts, and personality.

The first thing Gina did was to put her arm around Sandra and say, "We love you and God loves you. You know that, don't you?" Sandra nodded tearfully. "And you know that you will have to be punished for stealing and lying, don't you?" she said kindly. Sandra nodded again, her hands trembling slightly as she creased the folds on her dress.

"Remember when you asked Jesus to be your Lord and Savior?" asked Thad. They had often talked about faith in Christ, so Sandra responded immediately, "You showed me the Wordless Book. It started with a dirty page for sin, then a red page for the blood of Jesus, a white page for me being washed from sin, and a green page for growing as a Christian," she said, adding quickly, "I feel like that dirty page. Will God forgive me for taking the jacket?"

"Of course," Thad and Gina said in unison.

"How can I be a Christian and take the jacket?" she blurted out, a puzzled expression on her face.

Thad explained, "God gave you faith, but it takes time for you to learn how to listen to His voice. That last page is green. It means that you grow gradually in your relationship with Jesus, just like a plant grows from a tiny seed."

When Sandra's parents had first used the Wordless Book to teach her about Christ's atonement for her sins, they were doing what any pastor or Sunday school teacher could have done. However, they knew that God gave to parents, not temporary teachers, the primary responsibility for discipling their children in the faith, because they are the ones who are there when their children experience the trials of life. Parents are the only ones who have the kind of love necessary to stick with children when they slip. They can keep showing them a better way.

Edith Schaeffer said, "If parents believe that they can offer their children only a few superficial minutes of the day and expect them to be morally, spiritually, and intellectually stalwart, they are sadly mistaken. Functioning as a 'relay of truth' requires continual sensitivity to daily opportunities to teach, and a commitment to 'togetherness.'"

Moses said,

These commandments that I give you today are to be upon your hearts. Impress them on your children. Talk about them when you sit at home and when you walk along the road, when you lie down and when you get up. Tie them as symbols on your hands and bind them on your foreheads. Write them on the doorframes of your houses and on your gates (Deut. 6:6-9 NIV).

Sandra's parents could have been angry, humiliated, or deeply grieved, but God gave them the grace to look beyond the event that had occurred to see an opportunity to teach a truth.

Building Traits of Character

After Thad and Gina reminded Sandra of the Wordless Book, they asked her to read aloud the first chapter in Peter's second letter. It contains powerful teachings about the traits of character that God builds into every Christian.

We have divided them into four main categories:

- *Workmanship* (goodness and knowledge): working hard to be good and to do God's will
- *Self-control* (perseverance and godliness): deliberately laying aside selfish desires
- *Relationship* (brotherly kindness): enjoying and liking other people
- *Restoration:* loving others deeply

In your appendix/packet you will find a family Bible lesson on building relationships.

Sandra's parents did not just lecture their daughter, however. They took into consideration who she was and how she listened and learned. They used the information obtained in the first chapters of this book concerning their daughter's level of motivation, gifts, personality, and preferred communication style.

Most parents know that they should encourage spiritual growth in their children, but they are not quite sure what that means or how to do it. They sometimes think their responsibility ends with reading an occasional Bible story and saying grace at meals.

Confusion about spiritual growth even exists in the church, because one leader emphasizes prayer, another Scripture, another good works, or another prosperity. Jesus said the most important element was none of these. He said the most important factor was "'Love the Lord your God with all your heart and with all your soul and with all your mind and with all your strength.' The second is this, 'Love your neighbor as yourself.' There is no commandment greater than these" (Mark 12:30-31 NIV). To the extent that you daily teach your children to do just that, they will make beautiful music with their lives.

The passage from 2 Peter 1 used by Thad and Gina actually uses the language of music to explain character development. As each person adds on character traits, the new does not supplant the old. Each one is added to another.

In a fugue, one musical voice enters with the theme and then other voices are added, each with its own unique variation on that theme. For the Christian, faith in Jesus Christ is the theme of our fugue. The voices added and blended harmoniously together are workmanship, self-control, relationship, and restoration.

Peter said that our theme music of faith is based on the righteousness of Jesus. Sin has no rightful place. In order to be restored to God, Sandra needed to repent and return the jacket to her friend.

Christ's righteousness is more than a legalistic moral code, however. Those who put on His righteousness are empowered with His divine nature. They are given the power to overcome temptation and live a godly life.

If Thad and Gina had simply sent off Sandra to be punished, they would have missed an opportunity to teach her and pray with her. Everyone needs help in the battle against sin. It is important that children never be left feeling helpless or alone in this battle. Parents can teach their children from their own experiences how to overcome the wiles of the devil (Eph. 6:11). That builds character.

Condemnation does not build character. Sandra needed a penalty as part of the instructional process, but she did not need to be made to feel like a failure. Character growth takes time. It is not an instantaneous impartation but a gradual growth of trust and ability to hear God's voice. Parents play a crucial role in this process. Without their active participation, it takes a miracle of God for children to mature in their faith.

Four Indicators of Character Growth

The four categories of character growth listed above—workmanship, self-control, relationship, and restoration, show up first in certain attitudes of young children.

Parents see beginning evidence of *workmanship* when their children pay attention to stories read aloud to them or carefully complete a project. Workmanship includes attentiveness, punctuality, diligence, efficiency, and, most important, a desire to know and do God's will. All are traits needed by a good steward.

Self-control appears when children begin learning how to take criticism and follow instructions without resisting authority, grumbling, or complaining. Self-control includes qualities like compliance, obedience, temperance, and peacemaking. These traits are necessary for the humility and meekness of God's people.

Children show early evidence of *relationship* when they warm up to people quickly, seem comfortable with both children and adults, and are willing to cooperate in group games and activities. Relationships require interpersonal strengths like tolerance, cooperation, and appreciation that will be needed in both family and school settings. Children who grow up without learning how to build relationships also have the greatest number of job failures, because they simply cannot get along with others.

Restoration appears when children show sensitivity to a parent who is distressed, even when the parent tries to hide his or her emotions, and when they willingly share their belongings. Restoration includes sensitivity, gentleness, supportiveness, and compassion. Individuals who have reached the level of restoration show heartfelt concern for family members as well as outsiders. They become bonded to others because they go beyond superficial concerns and deal with the deepest needs.

Some people encounter God in such a dramatic way that they experience a changed heart overnight, but most character growth takes a period of years. Jesus could have produced loaves of bread every time someone was hungry, but His usual plan was for the grain to grow from a seed and ripen in season. Most spiritual maturity proceeds in the same orderly way—disciples guided by disciplers. That is the kind of growth that endures.

Kind Deeds by Unbelievers

As you will recall from previous chapters, the highest level of motivation is Level 4. At this level, acts of kindness are done out of the purest motive, love for God, practicing Paul's exhortation to esteem others more highly than one's self. Christ's followers do not merely look out for their own personal interests, but also for the interests of others (Phil. 2:4).

It is possible for anyone, believer or unbeliever, to do kind deeds and appear to function periodically at Level 4. It is also possible for someone who is a Christian to backslide to the selfishness of Level 1. However, a corrupt tree cannot bring forth good fruit (Matt. 7:18). If you look at the life of someone who is a mature disciple of Christ, you will see a consistent pattern of Level 4 behavior. The love of God literally flows through him. However, if you look at the life of a non-believer who occasionally does good works, the fruit in some areas of his life will be rotten. It is not possible to be a "good tree" without Christ.

Good works alone are not enough to truly help a person in need. Jesus said, "Let your light shine before men in such a way that they may see your good works, and *glorify your Father who is in heaven*" (Matt. 5:16 NASB, emphasis added). Unless a good deed points someone to God, directly or indirectly, it is not good fruit. Nothing is more important than showing someone in need that God loves them and will always be available. No matter how well intentioned, good works done for any other purpose than the glory of God are wood, hay, and stubble. They will eventually be burned up because they teach the recipient to rely on human beings for help instead of pointing them to God.

Spiritual Training of Children

If parents want the traits of workmanship, self-control, relationship, and restoration to thrive in their children, they will have to actively promote it. Few would deny that it is the parents' responsibility to train up their children in the way they should go—spiritually, emotionally, and mentally. Simply hoping that Christ-like character will develop is not enough. Parents must purposefully plan activities to encourage spiritual growth in each child. God brings the increase, but parents (and others) must do the planting and watering.

The ability to obey the great commandments does not come automatically once someone accepts Christ as Savior and is spiritually regenerated (born again). The potential to love God and neighbor is instilled at that time, but fully activating that potential takes time. Fruit starts out hard and green. Only over a period of time does it become soft and succulent. A new Christian, including one who is a child, shows some immediate changes in his life, but only a mature Christian consistently demonstrates the fruit of the Spirit: love, joy, peace, patience, kindness, goodness, gentleness, faithfulness, and self-control (Gal. 5:22-23).

Taking care of God's seed (our children) is a purposeful, active endeavor. Fathers bring up their children in the training and instruction of the Lord and do not exasperate them (Eph. 6:4). Mothers raise children to become God's ministers (2 Tim. 1:5), regardless of their profession.

If you ever feel fearful or inadequate as you try to help your child grow spiritually, remember that "God hath not given us the spirit of fear; but of power, and of love, and of a sound mind" (2 Tim. 1:7 KJV). With God's power, love for their children, and a sound plan for their children's growth, parents can accomplish their most important mission: training children to love and obey God.

Character Growth and Personality

Each individual has an easier time developing one character trait than another, because it comes along with the personality style. Perhaps this example will demonstrate what we mean.

School was out for spring vacation, so Francene invited girlfriends from her ninth-grade class to spend the night. All of them were essentially Level 3, responsible adolescents primarily motivated by their peers but also demonstrating strong character traits.

Sharion was the reliable member of the group. She asked Francene's mother to tell her the rules and then made sure the group followed them. Rolanda was cool, calm, and collected, demonstrating more temperance and patience than the others. She was flexible about what kind of music was played, but when things became too rowdy, she was the one to calm everyone down. Barbara was the social director. Outgoing and friendly, she tended to be the life of the party. Francene was not only the hostess, but was also the emotional barometer. She could sense if the joking and teasing were out of hand or personally hurtful. If one of her friends opened up about her parents, teachers, or boyfriend, Francene was the one who encouraged discussion. She also made sure everyone was having a good time and insisted on a consensus about what activity to do next.

Can you match each girl with the character trait she demonstrated? Try to decide before you go on.

Sharion, you may have guessed, demonstrated workmanship traits. Rolanda was self-controlled and Barbara showed relationship abilities. Francene practiced restoration.

These personalities have an affinity to each of the character traits:

Ruler	Workmanship
Designer	Self-control
Promoter	Relationship
Server	Restoration

Because one trait is dominant, each person with a certain personality style will have to make a conscious effort to develop the other three. This includes praying for those spiritual gifts that do not come naturally.

When someone lacks the character trait of restoration, for example, he should pray to the Father for the gift of Mercy. The Mercy gift equips one to function in a caring, sincere, and comforting fashion.

That is why a growing personal relationship with Jesus is so important. Through the work of His Spirit we are empowered to demonstrate all the elements of His character.

Believers can move from character that is shallow to that which has great depth if they take these three steps:

1. *Refuse to conform to the world* (Rom. 12:2).
2. *Pray for the gifts* (Matt. 7:7; 1 Cor. 14:1,12).
3. *Be doers of the word, and not hearers only* (James 1:22,25).

Character Transformation in Children

Moses exhorted the children of Israel to *hear, learn, keep, and do* the "laws and precepts" (Deut. 5:1). Parents can make sure their children *hear* from the word of God by reading stories about people who demonstrate character traits they need to develop. Children learn by memorizing verses and demonstrating that they understand them. Parents help their children to *keep* what they learn by "encircling it with hedges"—teaching them to remember, protect, and value what they hear in God's Word. Most children can "talk a good story" but *doing* what is right is more difficult. Parents can help children practice the character traits by taking advantage of daily situations, as in the story about Sandra, and by playing games like role playing. The Bible lesson in your appendix/packet uses these four building blocks. You will also find a list of Scripture verses for the family to look up to help them understand how God uses the various character traits.

Peter closed his letter about character growth with these words:

Be on your guard so that you may not be carried away by the error of lawless men and fall from your secure position. But grow in the grace and knowledge of our Lord and Savior Jesus Christ. To him be glory both now and forever! Amen (2 Pet. 3:17- 18 NIV).

CHAPTER SEVEN

SELF-ESTEEM

"Strike Two!" roared the umpire.

"Come on, Blake!" howled a voice from the bleachers. "Why doncha watch out for the fast ball!"

Blake looked helplessly toward his father's voice with a trace of fear on his chubby ten-year-old face. Just as he turned back toward the pitcher a fast ball whizzed past him down the middle of the plate.

"Strike Three! Yer out!" hollered the umpire.

"Oh no!" Blake's father shouted. "Not another strike-out, Blake!"

The boy lowered his head and headed for the bench, dragging his bat behind him. Coach Gabe gave him a friendly punch and said, "Hey, no problem, Blake. This guy's throwing fire today. He's killing us. We'll get him next time." As

114

Blake walked away, the coach looked up into the stands and saw Blake's father, Sid, still fuming and making remarks to the hapless people around him.

By the time the game was over, Blake's team had lost 13 to nothing. As people headed for home, the coach intercepted Sid. "Tough game," said Sid, with a disgusted look on his face. "I sure wish that kid of mine would learn how to hit a fast ball and not be such a ninny. He's chicken. The pitchers intimidate him. His brother Rick has no problems, but Blake . . ."

Gabe interrupted the string of complaints. "Sid," he said, "that pitcher was tough today. The whole team had a hard time hitting him. Look, I've been meaning to talk to you about Blake."

"Give it to me straight, Gabe. Do you want to bench him or what?".

"No, it's more important than that," said Gabe carefully. "I think you're being too rough on him. Blake is a fine boy. You shouldn't compare him to Rick. They're different. Rick takes naturally to baseball and Blake has some fun with it, but his heart isn't in it. I think he does it mostly because he wants to please you."

Sid squinted at the coach. "What's wrong with that?" he said.

Gabe replied, "Nothing's wrong with a son wanting his parents' approval, but he's not getting it, at least not in baseball. All he seems to do is let you down." Sid was turning slightly red and his eyes were steeling. Gabe said, "Frankly, Sid, I'm concerned about Blake's self-esteem."

Sid exploded, "Don't give me that humanistic stuff! You and I go to the same church. You've heard the pastor warn about this self-esteem lie. It's Christ who is to live in us, not ourselves. If my boy's a Christian, which I think he is, he doesn't have to worry about self-esteem. He should know that Christ loves him and that's that."

Gabe waited patiently for Sid to finish, then he added, "Pastor's right that we can go overboard with it, but the Bible says we are to esteem others more highly than ourselves. How can we give away something we don't have? The more of the right kind of esteem we have for ourselves, the more we will be able to esteem others. We know we're somebody important because God loves us, not because we constantly get applause. But God uses adults to demonstrate His unconditional love and approval to children. Jesus opened His arms to the children, no matter what their batting average was."

A small smile tweaked Sid's face as Gabe continued. "Blake is an average ball player. He does O.K., but his main interest is in other things. I've heard him play the piano at church. He's super. Look, he's self-conscious about his weight anyway . . . ."

Sid finally was ready for the bottom line. "Look, Gabe, what do you want me to do? Stop coming to the games? Keep my mouth shut in the stands? What is it you want me to do?"

"First, relax," Gabe said, without dropping his gaze. "I can tell that Blake appreciates your coming to the games, but he needs to hear what he's doing right once in a while. Sometimes I think they should get a medal just for practicing and playing in 90-degree heat. And did you see him catch that fly ball? At home, let him know about the things he does well, especially when he has bad days like this one. Hug him once in a while just for being himself, not for anything special he's done. I'm glad God doesn't love me for the good works I do. He loves me because I'm His child."

Both men could hear Blake's voice coming into earshot. "Hey, Dad, I had a hard time finding you," he said.

"Sorry, son. I needed to talk to Gabe for a minute. Hey, that pitcher threw like a hurricane today. I don't think anyone could have hit him, not even Babe Ruth." He turned and winked to Gabe as he walked off, his arm around his son.

What Is the "Self?"

Sid's reaction to the word "self-esteem" is not an

uncommon one in the Christian community today. The elevation of the Self has become a symbol for all that is wrong with the world. Is it possible to recapture the biblical concept of self-esteem? We believe it is both possible and necessary if we are to prevent incidents like the one at the baseball field and uncounted others that are duplicated at all levels of life.

The Bible speaks of the self in both positive and negative terms. Paul urged the church, "Offer yourselves to God" (Rom. 6:13 NIV). He also warned, "A bishop must be blameless, . . . not self-willed" (Titus 1:7 KJV). Jesus said to "Love your neighbor as yourself" (Matt. 19:19 NIV). Who is this self that we are supposed to love yet keep under control?

The self is that person you became at the moment of conception. God says it is of great worth: "I have called you by name; you are Mine! . . . You are precious in My sight" (Is. 43:1,4 NASB). He warns us not to despise ourselves:

> *Woe to him who quarrels with his Maker. . . Does the clay say to the potter, "What are you making? Does your work say, "He has no hands"? Woe to him who says to his father, "What have you begotten?" or to his mother, "What have you brought to birth?"*
> (Isaiah 45:9-10 NIV).

It is wrong to hate yourself, and it is also a sin to be prideful. No one can take credit or blame for his body features, intelligence, or accomplishments. It is God who makes us who we are.

The concept of self undergoes a number of changes in the process of progressing through the motivational levels. At Level 1, the self is the center of the universe. At Level 4, it has become something to be offered to help others. Peter wrote of Christ, who made the ultimate sacrifice of self, "He Himself carried our sins in His body up to the cross, that we might die to sin and live to righteousness" (1 Pet. 2:24 NASB). Because of His sacrifice, those who follow Him are empowered to die to the sin of self-centeredness and live in the righteousness of self-sacrifice. The true self does not have to be destroyed in the process. Because the self has worth, when the self is sacrificed, a great price has been paid.

The four stages of growth from self-centered to self-sacrificing correspond to motivational levels 1 to 4. They could be described as follows:

Self-centered: making the fulfillment of one's personal needs the highest priority.

Self-reinforcing: building up oneself by looking for compliments.

Self-respecting: finding affirmation in the respect of others.

Self-sacrificing: knowing who you are in Christ and copying His example. As Paul wrote,

> *Do nothing out of selfish ambition or vain conceit, but in humility consider others better than yourselves. Each of you should look not only to your own interests, but also to the interests of others. Your attitude should be the same as that of Christ Jesus"* (Phil. 2:3-5 NIV).

If parents want their children to progress from self-centeredness to self-sacrifice, to learn what it means to forsake all and follow Christ, they will have to make building their children's self-esteem a full-time job.

In this book, we define self-esteem as the opinion a person has about his purpose and worth. His opinions of himself vary according to setting and circumstance. For example, Blake, in the opening story, probably had a better image of himself as a pianist than he did as an athlete. He might consider himself "smart" in one area, such as history, but "dumb" in another area, such as math. These self-evaluations have a profound effect on a person's behavior.

Parents need to understand that developing a child's self-image is a crucial part of the parenting/discipling process. When a person is unsure of his identity and purpose, he will expend much energy trying to "find himself."

In *His Image/My Image* Josh McDowell summarized the importance of self-esteem when he wrote:

> *If you see yourself as a failure, you will find some way to fail, no matter how hard you want to succeed. On the other hand, if you see yourself as adequate and capable, you'll face life with more optimism and perform nearer your best.*

Parents play a large part in helping a child to see himself as a capable person. They express love and assure the child that God loves him. They also provide the tools that he needs to succeed. Knowing that God loves us, that we are joint-heirs with Christ, and that we are using His gifts for His purposes is the essence of a mature Christian's self-esteem.

Building the right self-esteem is an ongoing process. Our children are at various stages at different times. The next section will help you identify where your child is now and show you how to help him progress.

Levels of Motivation and Self-Esteem

The following summaries explain how individuals at each level of motivation determine their self-worth and suggest how parents can contribute to building them up. In the process, they will be helping their children progress to each new level, and ultimately to the most Christ-like level, Level 4.

LEVEL 1

Child determines his self-esteem by: how consistently his immediate needs are met; his ability to feel safe and secure.

Self-esteem increased by: faithful attention by parents and successful process of bonding.

Characteristics of Level 1 individual: He is self-centered and often unable to understand another's viewpoint. He makes frequent changes of activity because his interests are short-lived. When he tries something new, he wants to either do it his own way or make sure he gets something out of it. When his needs are not met quickly, he becomes upset.

The most natural Level 1 individual is the infant. In a healthy family, God provides for a baby's need for self-esteem through the bonding process that occurs between a child and his parents. The first parent a child bonds to is usually the mother. Magid and McKelvey describe the process in four steps:

1. The infant has a need, such as hunger or loneliness.
2. He communicates the need in the only way he knows how—a "rage" reaction, such as crying.
3. The need is met when the parent feeds or holds the child.
4. When the cycle is completed successfully over a period of time, the child develops trust.

Parents build trust as they consistently meet the child's needs, providing an essential building block for future healthy relationships with other people and God. Both psychologists and theologians have remarked on the emotional and spiritual significance of this bonding process. They have also sounded a dire warning about the effects of poor bonding or no bonding at all.

Infants raised without being bonded to their parents become detached and grow up trusting no one. Observers of institutionalized day care, for example, have noted that young children routinely dropped off begin to exhibit blank expressions.

In later life, children who have never experienced the bonding process tend to keep all their relationships superficial. In extreme cases, they grow up to commit heinous crimes because they have never developed a conscience. All they can do is act out the rage and anger that were never remedied when they were infants. They seek self-esteem at the most basic level, and it is never satisfied. God is able to intervene and help these people, but most of them have hardened their hearts during the survival process and do not respond. They feel so worthless they don't even think God could love them.

Individuals can bond later in life, but it is more difficult. Being available to meet the infant's needs is critical to the self-esteem building process. This means that one parent, usually the mother, needs to be available during the first year or two to carry out bonding. If you are a single parent with an infant or both parents must work, ask God to provide what you cannot, and remain open to His leading.

TRANSITION TO LEVEL 2

Once trust is firmly established through the bonding process, the most important activity for encouraging growth in self-esteem is to teach obedience, all the while reaffirming to your child that his needs will be met.

Parents of Level 1 children can do a number of activities with their toddlers to build self-esteem. These include:

- Setting simple rules for each time of day (meal-time, playtime, bedtime, etc.).
- Expecting simple responsibilities or duties to be fulfilled.
- Providing an agreed-upon reward or privilege when the rules are obeyed or chores are carried out.
- Providing negative consequences leading to re-pentance when a rule is broken. (See chapters nine and ten.)
- Maintaining an atmosphere of love, forgiveness, and acceptance where all basic needs are con-sistently met.

Sally knew that she was expected to pick up her toys after playing with them. When clean-up time was approaching, her mother would give her advance warning by setting a timer. When the timer went off and the toys were put away, Sally and her mother enjoyed a picture book together in the big chair. When the toys were not put away, Sally lost her reading time. She also could not play with another toy or move to another activity until her job was done.

If Sally became angry or upset, her mother would reassure her of her love but restate the rule and consequences. Next time, when Sally followed the rules, she would see that obedience has its advantages.

In addition to this process, Sally's mother used words and stories from the Bible to encourage her daughter to be obedient. They would repeat together, "Children, obey your parents, for this is the right thing to do," and her mother would explain that good things happen when people obey. When people don't obey, unpleasant consequences are bound to occur.

The Bible is packed with examples of rewards for obedience (Daniel, Joshua, Caleb) and punishment for disobedience (Jonah, children of Israel, the evil kings of Israel and Judah). Sally's mother read a Bible story about obedience each day during the time when she explained Sally's responsibilities. When Sally disobeyed, her mother led her through a prayer of repentance and ended their time together with a hug.

At Level 1, the processes of building self-esteem and developing discipline are closely intertwined. The goals are:

- Teaching children that the ultimate goal for a child of God is obedience.
- Establishing the bedrock on which parents build their children's character.
- Laying the foundation for the Spirit-filled life.
- Establishing habits of productivity.
- Learning about right relationships.

Beware of one hazard. Some adults view children motivated at Level 1 as evil creatures, needing stern, even harsh discipline. It is true that Level 1 children (or adults) are the epitome of selfishness and may need direct, intrusive correction. However, they are still God's precious creation. They may be the next generation of apostles, evangelists, and priests. God has endowed them with gifts, and He has a profound purpose for their lives. Any over-concentration on correction may produce what Dobson calls "breaking the spirit and the will."

If you are open to the Holy Spirit, you will often know when it is best to show mercy and when to correct. The gift of Mercy allows an adult to be patient and forgiving. The gift of Prophecy enables him to speak the truth. The ultimate goal is to speak the truth in love. This can only be accomplished when the parent is at high levels of motivation.

The best place to build positive self-esteem for Level 1 children is in an environment where parents love and enjoy their children while expecting them to obey. If you love your children as unique individuals that God created, you will instill in them a sense of purpose and worth that will last a lifetime.

LEVEL 2

Prerequisites for advancing to Level 2: bonding to parents and understanding of obedience.

Child determines his self-esteem by: his ability to please others as well as himself; the consistency of his relationships.

Self-esteem increased by: receiving approval for his efforts regardless of results; being loved unconditionally; being recognized for his worth as a unique child of God.

Characteristics of Level 2 children: They still want to please themselves but are now willing to seek the approval of people they trust. Unless bonding and obedience training have taken place, these children may be reluctant to enter the approval-seeking stage. They may be distrustful and lack the self-control necessary to learn how to please others.

This is a crucial stage. As a child grows he must receive appropriate approval for who he is and what he does. Otherwise, he will continue to seek the approval of others indefinitely, often in ways that are inappropriate. If a child does receive what he needs to build his self-esteem, in future years he will have the confidence to reach out and express approval to others.

At Level 2, individuals need to be commended for their efforts, not just their results. They need to know that they are good at something, that they have the ability to win praise and attention.

Parents and other adults should praise children for trying out new skills and making use of their gifts and personality traits. Be enthusiastic if your Level 2 Ruler sets up a lemonade stand or your Promoter puts on a play for the family. Express appreciation to your Server who sets the table without being asked, or your Designer who suggests how the family can get to church on time. The lemonade business may go sour, the play may flop, the table may be set with three forks and no knives at each place, and you may get to church late anyway . . . but they tried. They used the gifts and talents God gave them— not with the most mature intentions, perhaps, but they put forth the effort just the same.

Jesus showed unconditional approval to children, even praising them in front of crowds of people. However, He admonished the adult leaders of His day because they had never outgrown their need to seek the approval of man instead of God.

Transition to Level 3

Once your children have become established in the self-esteem they need at Level 2, they should be prodded to become mature in their motivation. God does not want them to make decisions indefinitely on the basis of their desire to seek the approval of others. At some point they need to reach a level where they seek only His approval and want to help others because of love, not a desire for their own advancement.

One way to encourage growth in self-esteem is to teach the child that God has given him gifts and talents to help others and to please God. Children as young as five or six can comprehend to some extent how God's gifts are used to help others in the body of Christ. (See Romans 12, 1 Corinthians 12, and Ephesians 4.)

Remember that following Christ's example means to esteem others more highly than ourselves (Phil 2:3). It is difficult to esteem others unless you know your own purpose and worth.

LEVEL 3

Prerequisites for success: previous experiences of gaining approval; knowledge of his worth as an individual; awakening of need to help others because of love for them and God.

Self-esteem determined by: competency; respect from family or group members; success of family or group through his efforts.

Self-esteem increased by: opportunities to use gifts in family or group; acknowledgements that he has been helpful to people or causes.

Characteristics of Level 3 children: The individual motivated at Level 3 desires respect more than overt verbal praise. He wants to know that he is not only part of the family or other group but also has an esteemed role there. He respects competence in himself and others and desires to achieve goals for the good of the group as well as for his own benefit. The Level 3 individual understands that his gifts can contribute to his family's happiness and harmony. He judges his worth by the degree of success he has in helping meet family goals.

If a Level 3 individual doesn't see a purpose for his gifts in the family, or he is thwarted in using those gifts, he will become discouraged. His self-esteem will be threatened and in time he will drop to a lower level of motivation.

Many family units are not functioning as they should in today's society. Divorce is a devastating blow at any age, but it is especially damaging to a child growing from Level 2 to Level 3. He feels like a failure because he was unable to halt the momentum of family breakup and may become reluctant to help others in the future.

Even without divorce, many families exist in such a dysfunctional state that individual growth is almost impossible. Members become so overwhelmed with their load of everyday details that they never consider the need for individual expression.

When children lack opportunities to use their gifts in the home, they will look for fulfillment elsewhere. They may sport unconventional hairstyles or wear bizarre clothes that identify them with a sub-culture.

Gangs thrive in the inner city because young men need to be part of a group that will use their talents for the group's benefit. Look for the individual who resists gang identification and you will see a healthy, supportive family, often with church and school activities close behind.

A commercial on television recently announced to parents, "Get your children hooked on sports, books, or music before they get hooked on drugs." There is much wisdom in that advice for all parents, but especially those with Level 3 children. The ad didn't mention it, but church youth groups are also a vital support to the family and a constructive opportunity for group activities. Even if the child is not fully committed to Christ, youth groups are excellent self-esteem builders and evangelical activities.

Adults in the church who are motivated at Level 3 tend to determine their purpose and worth by the degree to which they are allowed to use their gifts and talents for others. A wise pastor can help his members grow in self-esteem if he takes the time to find them a niche, a purpose, a channel for expressing their gifts. If they are allowed to be all they can be for the Lord, it will speed up the process of their spiritual development and greatly benefit the church at large.

LEVEL 4

Prerequisites for success: being loved and accepted; understanding his accountability to God and man; utilizing his gifts for the benefit of others.

Self-esteem determined by: presence of Christ in his life; degree of self-sacrificing service to others without thought of reward.

Characteristics of Level 4 children: At Level 4, individuals are motivated by doing what is right for others without thought of reward or recognition. They remain optimistic in difficult situations because they know that "God causes all things to work together for good to those who love God, to those who are called according to His purpose" (Rom. 8:28 NASB).

These people want to love God with all their mind, soul, heart, and strength, and to love their neighbors as themselves. They know that their worth is priceless, not only because of who or what they are, but because of God's love and grace.

As you will recall from the opening story, Blake's father thought that self-esteem would be supernaturally implanted in his son simply because he had made a profession of faith in Christ. In one sense, most new believers do immediately sense God's love, but the Christian life is more complex than that. God calls children, but he expects their parents to help them work out their salvation.

As a child, Blake needed to learn the nature of God by experiencing the love, acceptance, and discipline of his parents. Only then could he gradually grow to spiritual maturity. That is why it is so devastating when fathers provoke their children to wrath (Eph. 6:4), and why it is so wrong for mothers and fathers to abandon their families. These experiences stunt children's spiritual growth and put up barriers between them and God.

When a parent refuses to help his child grow in self-esteem, he is testing God. He is saying, "I'll let God do it," not out of faith but out of rebellion. God expects parents and adults to train a child in the way he should go, which includes building up his self-esteem. One tool that may help is the "I Love You" game in the appendix/packet.

The ultimate purpose for building self-esteem is for the child to love God and love his neighbor as himself. As people die to their own selfish interests, Christ brings alive in them power, love, and a sound mind. The more they give of themselves, the more they comprehend that it is not something they are doing but it is something done by Christ. When He lives in us, we can truly say we must decrease so Christ can increase. Only God can bring about this realization in us and produce the rich fruit of His love.

CHAPTER EIGHT

HOUSEHOLD TASKS: OPPORTUNITIES TO HELP

People come up with the most amazing excuses to avoid doing work. King Solomon liked this one:

The lazy man is full of excuses. "I can't go to work!" he says. "If I go outside I might meet a lion in the street and get killed!" (Prov. 22:13 TLB).

Why don't people like to work? Some say it is because God cursed man's labors at the Fall. However, God made work to be a blessing, not a curse. Sin destroyed it, not God, and so through Jesus Christ work can be redeemed.

Children who do work around the house learn several

valuable lessons:

- Obedience to parents
- Stewardship of the family home
- Organization of their time
- Teamwork
- Diligent application to a task
- Enjoyment of work

In addition, as children perform a variety of family chores, they and their parents discover interests that may suggest future careers. Children also learn that they do not need to fear the "lions" in the marketplace because they are building good work habits that will make them the valued employees of the future. With parental guidance, they will learn to view work as neither an evil nor an idol. It will become an opportunity to use the gifts God has given them in order to help others.

In this chapter, we want to help you understand the value of household chores and also give you practical guidelines for persuading your children to do their share. You will learn how you can match chores to your children's motivational level and personality, then help them choose the kind of tasks they will enjoy the most. You will also learn what to do about typical childish complaints and excuses.

First, here are a few basic guidelines to show you the difference between rebellious children who tear down a household and discipled ones who build it up.

How to Grow Rebellious Children

Ignore your child's motivational level and personality when giving orders for work.

Expect too much or too little.

Bark out orders and disappear.

Use household tasks only as punishments.

Do everything around the house yourself, grumbling loudly.

Wait until the child is at least ten years old before assigning chores.

Let your child skip his work every time he complains or makes excuses.

Always find something wrong with the way your child completes a task.

Talk about how much you hate housework.

Load on chores for the children while you sit around watching television.

Give your child money for making his bed and washing the dishes.

Provide no reminders about jobs that need to be done and scold loudly when anything is forgotten.

Never give praise for completion of routine work.

How to Train Disciples

Get to know your children as individuals.

Assign household tasks suited to each child.

Don't use everyday chores as punishments.

Start giving responsibilities beginning with the toddler age.

Give only short-term chores to young children.

Carefully teach skills and follow up to see that the work is completed.

Allow more mature children some flexibility in the way they complete their chores.

Provide charts and checklists to help your children keep track of their duties.

Praise every sincere effort to help, no matter how ineffective.

Find something good to say about the work even when explaining how it could have been done better.

Work alongside your children so they don't feel like slaves.

Emphasize the team approach to family chores.

Teach your children that God expects good steward-ship of the house and yard He has entrusted to your family.

Explain that the Bible says work is a blessing and an opportunity to serve God.

A number of years ago, all children had significant responsibilities around the home or farm. By the time they grew up, they had internalized proper attitudes toward work that carried over into their employment situations. As society has become more technologically oriented and full of labor-saving devices, children are no longer needed to keep the home in order. Parents are on the move so much they say "It's faster to do it myself" instead of giving instructions and follow-up to see that tasks are done properly. As a result, children no longer learn the value of being a contributing member of the family, let alone a contributing member of society.

We want to urge you to put your children to work in the home as soon as they are able. It is for their own good as well as the good of the family. The following list suggests respon-sibilities that most children can fulfill at various ages, beginning at ages two or three. If your children are past the age of ten, and you are just beginning to give them chores, we will show you how to approach that situation. Following this section you will find descriptions of how to achieve a higher success rate by assigning chores based on your children's gifts and personalities and learning how to deal constructively with their complaints and excuses.

Matching Jobs to Age Levels

Here are a few basic jobs your children can be ex-pected to do in the house and yard:

AGES 2-3
Bedroom: Return toys to proper place. Decide what to

wear from two choices. Undress self (still needs some help dressing). Kitchen and laundry room: Put napkins and silverware on the table, although not always in proper order. Take unbreakable dish to counter when finished eating. Help to wipe up own spills. Put away groceries on lower shelves. Living areas: Put magazines in a rack. Bathroom: Be toilet trained (between 2 and 3 1/2). Do simple hygiene, with help (brush teeth, wash hands and face).

Age 4

Bedroom: Make bed. Kitchen and laundry room: Set the table. Sweep with child-size broom. Load dishwasher or wash dishes (unbreakable ones). Follow a schedule for feeding pets. Help prepare simple foods: peanut butter sandwiches, simple desserts like gelatin and pudding, cold cereal. Hold hand mixer for cake mixes. Living areas: Share toys with friends. Dust furniture. Outside the house: Find specific items when grocery shopping. Give suggestions for grocery list. Help with yard and garden work. Tell parents destination before leaving house.

Age 5

Bedroom: Make bed and clean room (may still need help). Choose clothes for next day with parental guidance for occasion, weather. Learn to tie shoes. Kitchen and laundry room: Prepare food with supervision (sandwich, simple breakfast, juice, milk). Help prepare food for family (tear lettuce for salad, add ingredients for a recipe as directed, roll out cookie dough and cut shapes). Take out garbage. Sort laundry for washing. Fold and put away own clean laundry. Living areas: Answer phone. Make phone calls. Bathroom: Clean sink, toilet, bathtub.

Age 6-7

Bedroom: Hang up own clothes in closet. Master shoe tying. Kitchen and laundry room: Peel vegetables. Cook simple foods (hot dogs, toast). Clean kitchen. Carry in groceries. Living areas: Water plants. Bathroom: Leave bathroom in order. Outside the house: Water lawn and garden. Take pet for a walk. Bring in mail. Take out garbage.

Age 8-9

Bedroom: Clean own closet, drawers. Kitchen and laundry room: Set table properly. Mop floor. Prepare a simple recipe for a family meal. Living areas: Sew on buttons. Help with care of younger children (feeding, bathing, babysitting briefly with parent in the house). Polish furniture, silver. Bathroom: Take care of own bath/shower. Outside the house: Choose clothing when shopping with parents.

Age 10-12

Bedroom: Change bed linens. Kitchen and laundry room: Operate washer and dryer. Bake cakes, cookies. Clean oven and stove. Living areas: Write letters and thank-you notes without prodding. Plan own birthday party. Be alone at home. Learn handicrafts (embroidery, crocheting, weaving, knitting, woodworking, etc.). Outside the house: Earn own money (e.g., babysitting, yard work, paper route). Use own money for purchases, doing necessary computations. Wash the car. Clean pool and pool area. Mow yard.

In the packet you will find checklists you can use to help your children remember their duties and also give them praise. For the child who is too young to read, you can make a poster for the bedroom using pictures cut from magazines or catalogs. You could show a bed, a smiling face with lots of teeth, a toy box, etc., then print a single identifying word in large letters beside each picture (bed, teeth, toys, etc.).

Initiating Chores With an Older Child

If your children are ten or older and you are just starting them on household chores, the approach you use can determine whether their "help" brings harmony or chaos. Perhaps you can learn from one couple's experience.

Herb and Monica, like many American parents, had demanded little of their children in their early years. When their son Ben reached the age of ten, Herb called him into the den and said, "Mom and I think it's time for you to do more work around the house."

Ben's first thought was, "I wonder what I did wrong." He assumed that he was being punished unfairly for not doing the work all along. As a result, he became outwardly obedient to his father's demands but inside had a rebellious spirit.

Herb and Monica could have avoided this difficulty if they had assigned responsibilities to Ben at a young age as part of the discipleship process. They could have presented chores as an opportunity for Ben to help the family and grow into a person others could depend on.

Herb would have received better cooperation from his son if he had said, "Ben, your mother and I have been talking about how big you're getting and how you're taking the responsibility to feed the dog and clean your room every Saturday. We're proud of you. Every time you do something like that it helps the family.

"You're getting big enough to have even more responsibilities now. I was holding off until you were older but I think you can handle them now. What do you say? Want to give them a try?"

This approach would make Ben feel that his father was speaking to him as an adult, giving him an opportunity to become a respected member of the family.

Matching Work with Motivational Level

If Herb and Monica had understood how their son was thinking, they could have had a better chance of changing that thinking. One of the factors that gives understanding is knowledge of the child's motivational level.

For example, Level 1 and 2 children are still so

interested in meeting their own needs that they will see work as an interference in their little world. However, they are also developing the need for approval, and parents can use this to advantage. Parents can give frequent reminders that children who do their household chores are much appreciated because they are helping others and serving God.

At Levels 3 and 4, children respond best when they are entrusted with fairly complex decision-making about their work. They need less supervision and reinforcement and work harder when allowed to independently assume some responsibilities themselves. For example, during a Virginia Beach water shortage a few years ago, we were told not to flush toilets after every use and to restrict the number and duration of showers. My younger daughter Cindy, a Designer, immediately made up charts for when we flushed the toilet, when we took a shower, and how long it lasted. At the end of each day she reviewed each chart and made recommendations. She even tried to persuade us to use the facilities at the shopping mall, until we explained that although this would lower our water bill, it would have absolutely no effect on the water shortage.

Working with Different Personality Types

Here are general characteristics of each personality type that affect their attitudes toward chores:

Rulers can be persuaded to see chores as a challenge, particularly when given the freedom to make choices, such as when it is time to mow the lawn, when the house needs to be vacuumed, and so forth. To avoid anarchy in Rulers at lower motivational levels, however, give them checklists to mark off when completing each task.

Designers accept chores more quickly than others. They particularly like chores that allow them to make lists and to check things off.

Promoter children are just the opposite. They avoid chores whenever possible unless they can work in company with other people. The Promoter doesn't like working alone and doesn't like routine. At Level 3 or 4, Promoters will accept chores graciously, but unless they have opportunities for socializing, they will never really enjoy them. Chores are helpful to Promoters because they teach them self-control, a trait they badly need.

Server children assume responsibility to a fault. They want to do every chore in the house, particularly at lower levels of motivation. Since at lower levels their enthusiasm exceeds their ability, wise parents discreetly check up on the Servers' work, being careful not to hurt their feelings. Servers are fearful of public humiliation, especially at lower levels, so try not to give them tasks with high visibility. When they do fail and begin to make excuses, reassure them that they have not lost your love or confidence.

As you will recall from chapters two and three, within each child's personality style one or two gifts usually dominate. If you know what these gifts are, you can assign tasks accordingly, keeping in mind that each child should do a few chores that are not favorites, just because they need to be done.

PREFERRED CHORES (BY GIFT ORIENTATION)

Helping animals (M)
Helping people (M, G)
Running errands (M)

Organizing others and checking their work (P)
Working with others (M,S,E)
Working independently (G,T)
Competing with others (P,L)
Persuading others (E)

Doing boring or unpleasant chores (S)
Completing assigned short-term tasks (S,G,E)
Organizing long-term projects (P,L)

Working with details and complex tasks (T)
Experimenting with new methods (E)
Working with gadgets and machinery (S,G)
Working with paper and pencil (T)

(M = Mercy, G = Giving, S = Service, T = Teaching, E = Exhortation, L = Leadership, P = Prophecy)

Sally is a parent who did not take into account her son's personality style when getting him started on household chores. As a Designer, she kept such a neat house that a speck of dust never fell to the floor before she was in the process of vacuuming it up.

When Sally's son Derek was eight, she taught him to make his bed, fold his clothes, put his dirty clothes in the hamper, and pick up his toys. She went over the tasks carefully and taught him to do each one.

The first week on his own Derek did admirably. When Sally checked his room before school and at bedtime, everything was in place. The second week started well, but by Wednesday the bedclothes were sort of pulled up but not tucked in properly. Socks were in the chair by the desk. That night Sally called Derek to his room and asked him to explain.

Derek said, "Mom, I was running late for the bus, and if I didn't hurry, I would've been late for school."

Sally said firmly, "Tomorrow we'll just have to get you up earlier." After several weeks of these tactics, Sally became exasperated and began denying privileges to make him conform. It had little effect.

Derek seemed disappointed with himself each time, but unless he was closely supervised he wasn't able to do the job the way his perfectionistic mother desired. With a Promoter personality at about Level 2, he was somewhat disorganized and had little sense for detail. His concept of making the bed was to cover up the sheets, but not much more. He didn't even see the socks, or when he did, it was just too much effort to pick them up. Besides, in his eyes they didn't mess up the room. Regardless of what time he got up, he always dawdled before school. After school, his desire to rush out and have fun with his friends overrode his mother's instructions. He was always repentant, but the next day would have the same problems.

Derek's behavior would not have upset his mother if she had taken into account Derek's personality style and his low level of motivation. Because of his age and personality, he was unable to maintain his room the way his mother desired without daily supervision.

She could have speeded up Derek's learning process if she had put him on a reinforcement system using charts, stickers, and praise, along with a promised reward at the end of the week if he was able to keep his room clean. This would save his mother from nagging him, provide continuous incentives, and hopefully build good habits that last. It is worth observing, however, that Derek would probably never become a perfectionist like his mother.

DEREK'S CLEAN ROOM CHART

Rules: Pick up all toys and stuffed animals when not playing with them.

	Mon.	Tues.	Wed.	Thurs.	Fri.	Sat.	Sun.
Before School	X		X	X	X	X	X
Before dinner	X				X	X	X
Before bedtime		X	X			X	X
Before I play	X	X		X	X	X	X
After friends leave	X		X		X	X	X
Daily totals	4	2	3	2	4	5	5
Comments	Good start	Need to work harder	Better	What happened?	Much better	Wow!	Stupendous!

Handling Childish Complaints

It is inevitable. You will use all your best methods of persuasion and logic to present a list of chores to your children, and they will still complain about them. They will gripe about how much time chores take or how little their friends have to do in their houses. Or they will claim they have an unfair load compared to a brother or sister.

Most of these complaints just prove that "foolishness is bound up in the heart of a child" (Prov. 22:15 NASB). They don't know that you are trying to build their character, and they don't care. That is why God gave them parents like you to keep them in line until they see the truth for themselves. The qualities of workmanship and self-control they learn from household chores are essential for future success, but while they are still children, they will try to tell you from time to time that they would rather do without them.

Occasionally a complaint is justified, and a solution can be found even when it is delivered in a whiney, annoying tone of voice. The best approach is to correct the child's attitude and then deal with the issues. Children work better when they feel their parents are willing to listen to them, but they also need to understand that complaining for its own sake is displeasing to God and annoying to the family. Paul wrote, "Do everything without complaining or arguing" (Phil. 2:14 NIV). When the Israelites were in bondage in Egypt, God responded to their complaints and came to their rescue, but when they grumbled in the wilderness they incurred His wrath.

Part of the challenge of dealing with complaints is understanding not only the circumstances but also the type of person who has the gripe. Each personality type has its own style of complaining, so the parent can learn how to treat each complaint on an individual basis. The following summarizes the way children complain at the three lower levels of motivation and what you can do about it.

Rulers, especially at Level 1, come on strong and can be particularly offensive. Listen calmly and ask for suggested solutions, then politely but firmly tell them you need to look into the matter for yourself.

If the complaint concerns another child, don't take sides immediately. "Any story sounds true until someone tells the other side and sets the record straight" (Prov. 18:17 TLB).

Designers, especially at Level 1, are frequent complainers. They don't like interruptions and get upset if anyone disrupts the environment before their tasks are completed. Sometimes they have to let off steam by complaining about the enormity of the task because they have put too much pressure on themselves. This can be demoralizing to those around them.

When they come to you, listen to the complaint briefly but don't encourage self-pity or a martyr complex. Stick to the issues. Try to help them see the situation more clearly. You will avoid many complaints if you can give them work spaces where they will be free from interruptions and conflicts.

It also helps to praise their work as much as possible. Designers have fewer complaints and less depression if they feel they have parental approval for what they are doing. They fear failure and may begin to panic if they let their thoughts run away with them. Parental care and concern can often head off the hostilities brewing in their minds.

Promoters' complaints usually involve problems with other children. Parents should be friendly but encourage them to look at facts and issues, not personalities and opinions. Be alert to Promoters who have overheard others' complaints and repeat them in an attempt to win peer approval. Don't constantly reward your complaining child with words like, "You poor baby. That mean and nasty person was unfair to you." Insist that it is possible to promote harmony among all parties concerned. Jesus said, "Blessed are the peacemakers, for they shall be called sons of God" (Matt. 5:9 NASB).

Sometimes Promoters complain about other children just so they get the parental attention they need. Make sure you are giving them enough of your time.

Servers don't complain much to their parents, but they do like to repeat gossip that someone else has initiated.

Don't let them fall into that trap, but be alert to cases of legitimate complaints. Servers at lower motivational levels will often need your help in confronting an offending party according to Matthew 18.

Servers' complaints often result from their fears of rejection and criticism. They even fear rejection from their parents, so be careful to spend as much time as necessary to listen and show concern for their welfare. They may not express themselves well at first, and may even dissolve in tears, so parents need to be patient.

Constructive Complaints at Level 4

When complaints come from Level 4 children, the problems are usually legitimate and they have some ideas about resolving them. Level 4 Rulers rarely complain, and then only after they have thoroughly investigated a situation. Listen carefully because their suggestions are likely to be innovative and effective. Level 4 Designers are good sources of brief, accurate information. When they complain, there is usually something seriously wrong. They will usually make an effort to be completely frank with you. When their comments seem negative, they are usually in the process of working through the problem. Level 4 Promoters have keen insight and intuition. Their "people skills" are valuable in remedying problems in interpersonal relationships. Ask for their help. Level 4 Servers are usually adept at following the biblical model of confrontation and will proceed on their own initiative whenever possible. Conflict is still difficult for them, and it may be helpful for them to know you are available.

Any time your child comes to you with a complaint, it is always appropriate to pray. Jesus said if you have faith you can move mountains (Mark 11:22-24).

Those with complaints should look at their own motives. Jesus qualified that statement with another necessity: "When you are praying, first forgive anyone you are holding

142

a grudge against, so that your Father in heaven will forgive you your sins too" (Mark 11:25 TLB).

As your children grow, you will not always be there to help, but when they are young, your attentiveness and assistance model the love and ever-present help of the One who will never leave them.

Dealing with Excuses

If your child has done something that can be attributed to him and has found himself in trouble, you can almost guarantee that you will hear an excuse. That is because he wants to keep your approval.

Excuses are designed to accentuate the positives and minimize the negatives to keep up the image of perfection, even if it is a false one. Excuses save face and protect self-esteem.

Excuses are as old as Adam, who said, "It was the woman you gave me who brought me some [fruit] and I ate it" (Gen. 3:12 TLB).

Excuses were condemned by Jesus, who told of a servant who blamed his master when he was unproductive, instead of accepting the blame himself (Matt. 25:14-30).

Paul wrote that eventually "each one of us shall give account of himself to God" (Rom. 14:12 NASB). Parents can train their children to be better workers and prepare them for accountability to God if they teach them to stop making excuses.

As you disciple your children through household chores and tasks, try to maintain these attitudes:

- Wait until they finish speaking before you judge the merits of their excuses.
- Deal with the root of the problem.
- Counteract the need to make excuses with frequent praise and affirmation.
- Make sure your expectations are realistic.

Parents can listen to excuses with patience and love, but when dealing with unacceptable excuses, they should teach their children that:

- Excuses are often a sign of laziness.
- Reliance on excuses is a form of pride.
- Blaming others does not excuse actions.
- Fear of failure is never resolved by making excuses.
- Everyone is accountable to God.

You will find certain typical attitudes in excuse-making among the four main personality types.

Rulers like to disregard rules and directives if they conflict with their own goals. If their excuses are valid, give them any support they need to complete the tasks. If not, tell them firmly that you expect them to follow directions. Give a specific deadline and then follow up on it. Don't let the conversation focus on the excuse but on your expectations. If you accept their excuses and assign the work to someone else, you will be teaching them that excuse-making is a technique that works.

Rulers tend to be prideful, blaming people and circumstances but not themselves. They derive a sense of self-esteem from completion of tasks, so an inability to perform makes them feel like failures unless they save face with excuses. Steer them away from their anger and excuses into a non-threatening discussion of how they can realistically accomplish the required tasks. Affirm their ability to do the job, perhaps confiding ways in which you failed in the past and yet came back to succeed.

Designers are also task-oriented, but they don't make excuses as often as other personality types. Like Rulers, however, they tend to have their own agenda and may not always follow the assigned plan. They may also be unrealistic at setting deadlines for themselves. Because of their thoroughness, they may appear to be negligent about finishing their work on time when they are simply trying to do a good job.

Designers tend to blame themselves when they fail. Their excuses, even verbal ones, are almost spoken to themselves in an attempt to quiet the condemning voice inside. It relentlessly chides them for their inability to be both thorough and quick, or for taking any time off from the task at all. Some Designers will be the future workaholics.

Instead of blaming themselves for their inadequacies, Designers sometimes project their anger for their failures onto their parents. If you find yourself struggling with their resentment toward you as a harsh taskmaster, try to avoid conflicts over deadlines by anticipating delays and asking them for an honest evaluation of how long a task might take. Even then, explain that it is not always possible to anticipate the length of time it will take to complete a task. If you think it will help, build in some time padding to give the child a better chance to succeed. If you do this with Promoters, they will often slack off, but Designers will only be motivated to try harder.

Although they hate to admit it, Designers need your approval. It is important to overlook some of their hints at your incompetence as a leader (other than outright disrespect) and affirm their conscientious effort to do the job well.

Promoters make the most excuses of all the personality types, partly because they are so inefficient at completing their work. They spend too much time talking and clowning around. At first, instead of simply criticizing their failures, you can try steering them into checklists and other methods that will help them meet their deadlines. If that doesn't work, try breaking down the task into smaller pieces that can be completed one at a time, checking in with you at each stage for your approval. This will give them less control over their time and less opportunity to misuse it. It won't be a popular action on your part, but help them see that it is a step in the process of learning self-control. Warning: Don't pull the rope too tightly too soon.

Because Promoters want you to like them, praise is a powerful tool in motivating them to complete their work. Another aid is providing tasks with opportunities for using people skills. If their socializing proves too distracting, don't put them in solitary confinement, just teach them how to resist the temptation to ditch the job and fool around with their friends.

Servers fail at times because they never understood the assignment. After you give an explanation, have them repeat back what they have heard. If you make certain they know what is expected of them, you can reduce their number of failures and resulting excuses.

Among all the personality types, most children at Level 4 only make excuses when something is truly wrong. Therefore, it is important to listen carefully to what they say.

Level 4 Rulers almost never make excuses. Like the soldier trained to say "No excuse, sir," they have imposed on themselves the attitude that they should never shirk responsibility. They will also take the blame for a weaker sibling rather than point an accusing finger. Level 4 Designers have become more realistic about their working style and are able to set reasonable deadlines. They would rather burn out in the process of doing the job right than try to make excuses.

When a Level 4 Promoter makes excuses, they will be valid. You can trust this person's evaluation of the situation. Even if it appears that they "wasted" the afternoon talking to someone, for example, you can be assured that something important transpired. Being sensitive to human need, they are able to set aside what seems "urgent" and deal with the "important."

Level 4 Servers are also acutely aware of others' needs. Their remarks that seem like excuses are usually an attempt to show you the reasons for their decisions. They may still have difficulty with confrontation in attempting to get others to work together, but by this level most of them have internalized the ability to "self-talk" themselves into doing what is necessary.

Dealing with Outside Criticism

If you expect everyone in your family to participate in chores, beginning at the toddler age, don't be surprised if you are criticized. Outsiders who misunderstand your motives may think that children should be free from responsibilities in the home. Someone may say in your hearing, "When I see children taking care of their brothers and sisters, I wonder why they can't be outside playing with their friends. Caring for brothers and sisters during summer vacation is child abuse. Child labor laws should prohibit such things."

Certainly, if caring for brothers and sisters were the child's total existence, it would be wrong. But for a couple of hours a day it certainly is within the bounds of propriety, particularly if you as a parent know why you are giving your child such a responsibility and what you hope to accomplish. Household chores are a privilege, a rite of passage, not a punishment inflicted on helpless children.

The best way to respond to people who make negative comments is to explain that your family operates as a team to keep the house in running order. You use household chores as a method of discipling your children and building their character. Chores are a privilege and a stewardship responsibility, not a punishment or something to dread. Let the person know you understand the difference between using your children as indentured servants and expecting them to assume reasonable responsibilities. Your intention is not to deny your children their childhood, but to help them grow into the type of adult who will bring glory to God.

Use chores as a blessing, not a curse—for yourself and for your children. Check the appendix/packet for extra help on making this a reality.

Chapter Nine

Discipline and Discipleship

"You stop that or I'm going to spank you!"

That is the parental threat of the ages, but is it always justified? In truth, discipline means much more than "spare the rod and spoil the child." It means discipleship.

Deciding how to discipline a child is one of the most difficult tasks parents must face. It is only human to want a peaceful home. When children, young or old, are behavior problems, parents run the gamut from totally ignoring it to becoming absolutely furious.

When we speak of discipline problems, we are talking about misbehavior that occurs either deliberately or through omission. We must deal with both if we want our children to grow up to become responsible adults.

The best approach to discipline is to prevent as much

misbehavior as possible by taking the positive approach of emphasizing character development and rewarding good behavior. Children flourish under a well-planned discipleship upbringing.

The Bible says, "Fathers, do not exasperate your children; instead, bring them up in the training and instruction of the Lord" (Eph. 6:4 NIV). What does this mean? In the next few pages we will show you how it is possible to train and instruct a child "in the way he should go" so that "when he is old, he will not depart from it" (Prov. 22:6 KJV). We will review the characteristics of children at Levels 1 and 2, show what a child is trying to accomplish with his misbehavior, and then offer a variety of disciplinary methods available to parents according to the child's personality. Chapter 10 will deal with the special problems of disciplining adolescents and those at Levels 3 and 4.

Discipline for Children at Levels 1 and 2

As you will recall from chapter one, children grow through a series of stages that involve not only physical and mental growth but also maturing of the emotions and spirit. Here is a review of the first two levels of motivation as they relate to discipline:

LEVEL 1 CHILDREN
- Motivated by their basic urges
- Want their self-centered needs met before they will even consider the interests of anyone else
- Do not have the skills and self-discipline to perform tasks independently
- Function best in a structured environment
- Are unable to grasp reasons why certain acts are right or wrong
- Need parents and others to order their lives until the conscience is developed
- Obey primarily because it helps them avoid punishment

LEVEL 2 CHILDREN

- Need less structure even though they are still motivated by basic needs
- Desire to please others
- Don't respond well to nagging
- Behave best if given frequent praise, encouragement, and instruction
- Are becoming aware of the existence of universal moral standards
- Can comprehend some of the reasons why certain actions are right and others wrong
- Can begin developing an internal moral code, with parental help, that will guide them in the future

Goals of Misbehavior

What are children trying to gain by their misbehavior? Here are a few clues:

CHILD'S STRATEGY	CHILD'S GOAL
Annoyance	Attention
Intimidation	Power
Cruelty	Revenge
Helplessness	Assistance

Although children seem to be at war against their parents, their real battle is against the world of orderliness and kindness. They don't want to outgrow their self-centeredness and start considering the needs of others. Parents need to convince them—by a variety of means—that it is in their best interest to do so. In the process, they will be steering their children on a course from Level 1 to Level 4.

All parents know that they are supposed to intervene when their children misbehave, but not everyone agrees on how to do it. Husbands and wives bring to marriage certain beliefs about what behavior is "bad" and what is "good." They even have some ideas about how to regulate it. Unfortunately, many parents assume, erroneously, that their partners have the same ideas as they do and so they never talk about it. However, no marriage will be a partnership until a husband and wife agree. They must take time to discuss what goals they have for their children, what behavior is acceptable, and how this will be enforced.

We want to suggest to you the following corrective methods. They vary from gentle to severe, depending on the motivational level and personality of the child and the nature of his offense. Spanking is only one of the many methods useful for training a child. Dobson advises that it be reserved for cases of willful disobedience, as opposed to an accident, and not used on children over age ten.

The main purpose of discipline is not releasing anger, or getting even with the child for causing trouble, or even controlling unruly behavior so the home will be more peaceful. The main purpose is discipleship—loving instruction that will enable the child to "grow in grace, and in the knowledge of our Lord and Savior Jesus Christ" (2 Pet. 3:18 KJV).

With this principle of discipleship in mind, plan ahead to avoid putting children in a situation where they misbehave. Prevent rather than react. When action is needed, consider these basic guidelines for discipline:

GUIDELINES FOR DISCIPLINE
- Act quickly against misbehavior, unless you are too angry to act justly.
- Use the least intrusive method necessary to convince.
- Use a method that fits the crime and is appropriate to your child's personality and motivational level, even if it is not a method that comes naturally to you.
- Ask yourself, "What would Jesus do?"
- Make discipleship your goal, not control.
- Clear the way for restoration by concluding the time of discipline with prayer, hugs, and teaching.

- Never stop trying to lead your child in the paths of righteousness, gently but firmly.

It is important to understand these basic guidelines for godly discipline and also to have a variety of methods available for enforcing that discipline. The following methods vary from those that intrude the least on your child's activities— and yours— to those that intrude the most. In general, the child at Levels 3 and 4 will respond consistently to the least intrusive methods. At Levels 1 and 2, these methods have some success and are worth trying, but the more intrusive methods are often needed to get results.

Parents need to remain constantly aware of their child's current motivational level and personality so as not to impose disciplinary measures that are either too harsh or too weak. For example, Rulers and Level 1 children need stronger medicine than Servers.

Finally, parents need to consider their own motivational level and personality. Each parent may be more comfortable with one technique than another because of his personality style. However, parents cannot afford to do only what comes naturally. They need to take time to match their approach to the disciplinary needs of the child who is being discipled. For example, a Ruler parent will need to seek a gift of Mercy when dealing with a Level 3 Server child. A Server parent will need extra firmness when training a Level 1 Ruler child. The parent may need to ask for gifts of Prophecy or Leadership if he has not already received them.

We have divided discipline into these four categories: preventing, supporting, appraising, and controlling.

Preventing is the least restrictive on the child and takes the least amount of the parent's time. Supporting is a more active method where the parent asks questions and challenges the child's behavior. Appraising involves setting up a formal or informal agreement with children regarding acceptable behavior, rewards, and punishments. Controlling is the most intrusive action against the child and includes time-outs and spankings.

PREVENTING
Planned Ignoring
Control of Environment
Adult-Level Questions
Nonverbal Signals
Modeling

Planned ignoring. Many times, children will repeat a certain misbehavior because they know it is guaranteed to get their parents' attention. Unless it is disruptive to others, like a temper tantrum in a grocery store, parents may be wise to simply ignore it. Without an audience, the child may often decide it is not worth the effort.

Control of environment. Many children behave far better when their parents are close by and available than when they are distant and preoccupied. Much misbehavior can be avoided by the companionable presence of a parent. Parents who are available will also be able to notice which elements of the environment need to be adapted to remove temptation, such as moving breakable objects out of reach or placing forbidden sweets out of sight.

Adult-level questions. Sometimes it works better to address a child more as an adult than as a naughty child. Instead of saying, "Who made this mess?" or "Why do I always have to clean up after you?" try saying, "What can I get for you so you can clean this up?"

Non-verbal signals. Every parent develops a repertoire of certain looks (stern or approving), hand signals (pointing accusingly or applauding), and head shakings that communicate volumes without a single word being spoken.

Modeling. One of the best ways to teach your child good behavior is to behave well yourself. Be the kind of person you want your child to become. Tell them about Jesus and role models from the Bible as well as people you admire in your neighborhood and church.

SUPPORTING
Repetition of Rules
Positive Statements
Subtle Directives
Reflective Listening
Probing for Reasons
Self-monitoring

Repetition of rules. Spell out from five to seven house rules for your children so there will be no question about what is right and wrong. Repeat them daily. Explain consequences for breaking rules and make sure these penalties are carried out.

Positive statements. Children need to know that somebody who cares about them knows they are there. They will be less likely to misbehave if they consistently receive positive input from their parents. (See Philippians 4:8 for a biblical model of ways to accentuate the positive.)

Subtle directives. Sometimes children respond better to a request than a demand. Try asking, "Would you like to get back to setting the table now?" If this doesn't work, of course, the parents need to proceed to a more explicit demand.

Reflective listening. When your child makes an angry statement, reflect it back to him in different words. Show him what you see as the apparent meaning behind the message. If he says, "You're the meanest Mommy in the world!" respond by saying, "You're angry with me."

Probing for reasons. It isn't enough to enforce change in outward behavior. Children need to change on the inside, too. Your goals as parents are not only short-range relief of a problem but long-range training in proper behavior and attitudes.

Parents can sometimes determine the reasons behind their children's misbehavior by looking at their own reactions to it. Do you feel annoyed? If so, attention-getting is probably the goal. Try planned ignoring or another preventive strategy. Do you feel intimidated? The child is probably trying to usurp your authority. Do you feel wronged or hurt? He probably wants revenge. Help him resolve the conflict. Do you seem unable to reach him? He is probably feeling helpless and useless and needs opportunities to do something constructive around the house and yard.

Self-monitoring. If your child has difficulty maintaining good behavior over an extended period of time, help him set a series of short-term goals. Write each goal on a chart so that he can come to you to check it off. Set up a reward he can receive after meeting several goals in a row. For example, set a ten-minute goal for not whining. Promise him a small trinket for meeting his goal five times in a row. Obviously, you can't do this indefinitely, but it will help establish in his mind that good behavior pays off.

APPRAISING
Stopping and Redirecting
Logical Consequences
"What" Questions
Contracting for Positive Behavior
Token Reinforcement

Stopping and redirecting. At this point, the child knows he has been "found out." He hears you say that he is to stop his misbehavior and start doing what is right. Without a lot of fanfare and explanation, the parent says, "Don't do that; start doing this."

Logical consequences. Sometimes the best lessons are learned when a child is allowed to continue on his foolhardy course and find out where it leads him. This includes the inevitable imposition of a natural or logical penalty that he knew in advance would be the price paid for certain misbehavior. For example, if he has been warned twice about the position of his cup of milk but spills it anyway, have him clean it up.

"What" questions. "What are you doing?" forces a child to admit his misbehavior. A "why" question only invites excuses. The parent should continue repeating the "what" question until the child describes the misbehavior in his own words. At that point, they agree on a plan to stop the misbehavior, including a future penalty if it continues.

Contracting for positive behavior. Under this kind of contract, a child knows what he is expected to do and what rewards he can expect for each accomplishment. This positive approach releases parents from constant harping on negatives and gives them the freedom to encourage correct behavior.

Token reinforcement. Tokens are small acknowledgements of good behavior that can be accumulated for a tangible reward. Instead of giving out a prize for every correct behavior, the parent gives the child a sticker or check mark on a chart. At the end of the week, the stars or checks can be counted and an appropriate reward given. (Children at a low level of motivation may need a daily reward at first.)

CONTROLLING
Isolation to Complete a Plan
Time Out to Cool Off
Loss of Privileges
Spanking

Isolation to complete a plan. When a child persists in disruptive behavior, one result he should expect is a time of isolation from friends and family to prepare his own remedy for his misbehavior. He is not just waiting out his time as a punishment but is expected to find a way to help himself. He should ask, "What did I do? Why is it a problem? What rule did I break? What can I do so it won't happen again?" When he has arrived at an acceptable solution, he can return to the group again.

Time out to cool off. This is a penalty for an explosion of anger that cannot be dealt with using milder measures. No arguments are allowed. The offending child is sent or taken to his room or a neutral area like the laundry room where he waits out his time. Parents may want to set a timer so they will not be besieged with requests for clemency. If the child is not repentant and quiet at the end of the time, he may need an extended sentence. The parents would be wise to conclude the time out with a gentle lesson from Scripture and a time of prayer and reconciliation.

Loss of privileges. Sometimes a more lengthy penalty is required to communicate clearly that a child's infraction is a serious matter. He may be restricted from television for a day or more, or from playing after school or in the evening. Older children may temporarily lose rights to allowance or use of the family car. Be careful not to set such a lengthy term of restriction that the child becomes bitter and the parents become worn out from playing policeman. Usually the point can be made quite quickly.

Spanking. Give physical punishment only to a child who knowingly breaks a rule and is willfully disobedient. Administer this punishment privately. If you are too upset, send the child to his room first until you have prayed and calmed your anger. Explain why the punishment is necessary, administer it, then give comfort, consolation, and affection. Pray together and teach the child a principle from Scripture.

You will know your disciplinary measures have been successful when true repentance and restoration take place. That is the time when parents should do what God does with the memory of our sins— He forgets them. Start your child with a clean slate from that moment on. Unless your child repeatedly commits the same sins, do not bring up unrelated offenses again.

Andrea Lee is a six-year-old girl who has a Designer personality and is operating at Level 2. Recently she has been leaving her toys all over her room. Robert and Sylvia, her parents, must remind her constantly to pick them up. They both realize that constant reminders are not sufficient, so they check the chart and see that for her level and personality a Supporting strategy is recommended for the best results.

Before intervening, they decided to complete a problem-solver worksheet (you will find one in your packet). This is how Andrea Lee's worksheet looked after her parents were finished with it:

PROBLEM-SOLVER WORKSHEET FOR PARENTS

Name: Andrea Lee
Personality: Designer
Level of Motivation: Level 2
1. *What is the misbehavior?* Andrea leaves her stuffed animals and her playthings wherever she last played with them in her room.
2. *What corrective strategies have you tried?* We try to remind her to make sure her room is picked up before she goes outside or before dinner, etc. We have restricted her from going outside when we have checked the room and it isn't picked up.
3. *Have you been successful?* When we remind her, she goes back and does it, but she fusses if her friends are waiting. When she can't go out, she cries and promises she will do better next time. The improvement lasts for two or three days, and then we start the old routine again.
4. *What are the general categories for the methods you have tried?* Control of environment (preventing strategy). Stop and redirect (appraising strategy). Restrictions (controlling strategy).
5. *Do you believe it is time to use another strategy? Why? Which strategy will you try next?* Yes. We have been inconsistent and not developed a plan. We have only controlled but not taught her anything. We should try the supporting strategy and be more consistent.
6. *How will you implement the strategy?* Of the choices under the Supporting category, repeating the rules would probably be the best. At Level 2 she is more forgetful than rebellious. We haven't focused on the neat room enough, either. She might delay her time with her friends if we gave her lots of approval. As a Designer, it is pleasing to her to have an orderly room. She would also respond well to charts and could monitor herself. We could give her lots of praise for all her check marks.
7. *What character traits are needed to help you solve the problem?* Orderliness, planning, responsibility, diligence.
8. *If behavior improves, what strategy will you use?* We will decrease the review of rules and check the chart only once a week. We will continue to say nice things about what she is doing.
9. *If behavior doesn't improve, what strategies will you try?* Probably the logical consequences and possibly a contract or token rewards.

The strategy that we used to solve Andrea Lee's problem can be used for any child six to sixteen. It is important to use age-appropriate interventions and to take into account personality and level of motivation. Keep in mind the following:

- Recall what you have done before that was successful.
- Determine what strategy is suggested by the chart.
- Before you have a crisis, learn how the different strategies work.
- Decide to disciple, not punish.
- Give the strategy a fair trial before deciding if it will work.
- Review regularly what you are doing and thinking.

Teach your child that you are not adversaries but members of a family who only want the best for one another. Using this story as a model, work through your child's behavior problems by filling out the form in your packet. At all times keep in mind that your goal is not control but discipleship.

Design for Discipleship

The following chart will help you decide which strategy is appropriate for the typical misbehaviors all parents encounter. Once you find your child on the chart, you can design a unique plan of discipline for him based on his personality and motivational level.

The abbreviations listed under each motivational level refer to the groups of strategies described: P = Preventing; S = Supporting; A = Appraising; C = Controlling.

BEHAVIOR MODIFICATION PLAN
RULER

BEHAVIOR PROBLEM	BEST STRATEGY FOR EACH MOTIVATIONAL LEVEL			
	LEVEL 1	LEVEL 2	LEVEL 3	LEVEL 4
Angry outbursts	C	A	A	A
Arguing	C	A	S	P
Bad language	A	A	S	S
Chores poorly done	C	A	S	S
Curfew-breaking	C	A	S	S
Defiance	C	A	A	A
Destruction of property	C	A	A	A
Excuse-making	C	A	S	S
Grades poor	C	A	S	S
Hitting	C	A	A	A
Lack of motivation	C	A	S	S
Lying	C	A	S	S
Room messy	C	A	S	S
Silliness	C	A	S	P
Speeding	C	A	A	A
Stealing	C	C	C	C
Talking excessively	C	A	S	S
Tantrums	C	A	A	A
Tattling	C	A	P	P
Toys lost or mistreated	C	A	S	S

P = Preventing; S = Supporting; A = Appraising; C = Controlling

Behavior Modification Plan
Designer

Behavior Problem	Best Strategy for Each Motivational Level			
	Level 1	Level 2	Level 3	Level 4
Angry outbursts	A	S	S	S
Arguing	A	S	P	P
Bad language	A	S	S	S
Chores poorly done	A	S	S	S
Curfew-breaking	A	S	S	S
Defiance	A	A	A	A
Destruction of property	A	A	A	A
Excuse-making	A	S	S	S
Grades poor	A	S	S	S
Hitting	A	A	A	A
Lack of motivation	A	S	S	S
Lying	A	S	S	S
Room messy	A	S	S	S
Silliness	A	S	P	P
Speeding	A	A	A	
Stealing	C	C	C	C
Talking excessively	A	S	S	S
Tantrums	A	A	A	A
Tattling	A	S	P	P
Toys lost or mistreated	A	S	S	S

P = Preventing; S = Supporting; A = Appraising; C = Controlling

BEHAVIOR MODIFICATION PLAN
PROMOTER

BEHAVIOR PROBLEM	BEST STRATEGY FOR EACH MOTIVATIONAL LEVEL			
	LEVEL 1	LEVEL 2	LEVEL 3	LEVEL 4
Angry outbursts	A	A	A	A
Arguing	A	A	S	P
Bad language	A	A	S	S
Chores poorly done	A	A	S	S
Curfew-breaking	A	A	S	S
Defiance	A	A	A	A
Destruction of property	A	A	A	A
Excuse-making	A	A	S	S
Grades poor	A	A	S	S
Hitting	A	A	A	
Lack of motivation	A	A	S	S
Lying	A	A	S	S
Room messy	A	A	S	S
Silliness	A	A	S	P
Speeding	A	A	A	A
Stealing	C	C	C	C
Talking excessively	A	A	S	S
Tantrums	A	A	A	A
Tattling	A	A	S	P
Toys lost or mistreated	A	A	S	S

P = Preventing; S = Supporting; A = Appraising; C = Controlling

BEHAVIOR MODIFICATION PLAN
SERVER

BEHAVIOR PROBLEM	BEST STRATEGY FOR EACH MOTIVATIONAL LEVEL			
	LEVEL 1	LEVEL 2	LEVEL 3	LEVEL 4
Angry outbursts	A	S	S	S
Arguing	A	S	P	P
Bad language	A	S	S	S
Chores poorly done	A	S	S	S
Curfew-breaking	A	S	S	S
Defiance	A	A	A	A
Destruction of property	A	A	A	A
Excuse-making	A	S	S	S
Grades poor	A	S	S	S
Hitting	A	A	A	A
Lack of motivation	A	S	S	S
Lying	A	S	S	S
Room messy	A	S	S	S
Silliness	A	S	P	P
Speeding	A	A	A	A
Stealing	C	C	C	C
Talking excessively	A	S	S	S
Tantrums	A	A	A	A
Tattling	A	S	P	P
Toys lost or mistreated	A	S	S	S

P = Preventing; S = Supporting; A = Appraising; C = Controlling

Control vs. Discipleship

We have used the contrasting terms control and discipleship several times in this chapter. Discipleship as presented here is an ideal that few parents attain all the time, but they can always strive toward that goal. It is practiced consistently by the Level 4 parent who is at peace with himself and God, willing to sacrifice time and effort for the good of his child. Here are the two extremes:

CONTROL	DISCIPLESHIP
Child treated like prison inmate	Child treated like beloved treasure
Child is always motivated by fear	Child obeys out of love and respect
Child's independence stifled	Child develops confidence
Talkative child criticized as chatterbox	Child always finds a listening ear
Order kept in the home so parents have peace and quiet	Child disciplined so he will grow toward Christlikeness (Level 4)
Punishment is unpredictable, varying with the needs of the parents	Discipleship is consistent, guided by house rules with appropriate consequences and love
Parent acts in anger; may have difficulty recovering love feelings	Parent is angry but does not sin; never stops loving; works by a plan

Parental Unity

When discipleship is occurring in a home, there is usually a high degree of agreement between the parents about how to raise their children. In homes where children are presenting serious behavior problems, we have found that parents have usually been in disagreement concerning their expectations for their children. Many couples have never sat down and discussed their goals for their children or decided on methods of discipline that both agree they will use. They may be deliberately or inadvertently contradicting each other by using opposing methods with the child. It is nearly impossible for children to thrive in a home like that, and the marriage suffers damage as well.

Here is a story about one family's experience.

Maria said angrily to her husband, "Don't you think an hour of drills is a bit much for a six year old?"

Angelo responded hotly, "Absolutely not. How else do you expect him to master these skills?"

"Look," said Maria, "the poor kid has been in school all day and he did a half hour of homework. What more do you want?"

Johnny cringed. His parents were always fighting over him. Ever since Johnny started first grade, his father had been drilling him on every new subject his teacher covered. Lately he had been introducing material of his own. Johnny wanted to please his father, but by the end of the day, he was so tired he couldn't focus on all the drills his father kept pushing at him. As a result, almost every night Angelo would start the drills, become exasperated with his son, and send Johnny to bed in tears.

Maria tried reasoning with her husband, but it only made him more determined. When she criticized him, he shut her out. Ultimately, the situation became so tense that it affected every area of their relationship.

Angelo and Maria came from widely different backgrounds. Angelo grew up in an overly strict home where his parents were firmly in control. Although he resented the way his parents treated him, he unconsciously adopted many of their strong-arm tactics when dealing with Johnny.

In Maria's family, the children had a lot of freedom.

Her parents took time to listen to their children and teach them the difference between right and wrong. When they misbehaved, the parents talked to them, brought them to repentance, and then administered the appropriate penalty.

Angelo and Maria had never discussed how to discipline their children. When they talked excitedly about starting a family, they assumed that everything would take care of itself. The first sign of trouble occurred when they disagreed on toilet training. Angelo told Maria she was too permissive and should scold Johnny every time he wet his pants. Maria thought Angelo was unfair, so she privately resolved to counteract what she saw as his mistreatment of Johnny. She rarely scolded her son for anything, and since she was the only one home during the day, she handled the discipline pretty much her own way.

When Johnny went to school, Angelo became more involved, and that was when the real fights started. Convinced that their marriage was coming apart at the seams, Angelo and Maria sought out their pastor.

It took several sessions before the pastor realized that the issue that had sparked the marital problems was Johnny's extra-practice sessions. "Have the two of you ever sat down and talked about your expectations for Johnny or your methods of disciplining?" he asked. To his amazement they both said "No." Neither had ever realized that although they both wanted the best for Johnny, their family backgrounds had given them opposite notions of how that should be achieved.

Angelo focused on preparing for the future, believing that tough practice sessions were essential if Johnny were to be successful in life. Maria focused on a strife-free present. She looked for ways to make Johnny happy and frequently excused his misbehavior.

The pastor told them gently that both of them were a little right and a little wrong. He explained to Angelo that all children pass through a series of developmental stages. These include not only physical changes like the gradual increase in fine muscle control, but also the growing ability to think abstractly and handle complex tasks. At age six, Johnny didn't have the physical stamina for his father's nightly drills. Also, he had not yet reached the stage where he could focus on any one task for a long period of time or master the type of reasoning that his father demanded.

Maria was more sensitive to Johnny's needs, but her expectations for her son weren't as high as they should be. Often she made life a little too comfortable for him by not demanding that he stretch to reach new heights.

Angelo had assumed that disciplining Johnny meant control—whatever it took to keep him in line. With the help of his pastor he was released from that straitjacket to be Johnny's loving teacher instead of his prison guard.

At the pastor's direction, Angelo and Maria spent some time alone together and set goals for Johnny in the following areas:

- Health habits
- Family relationships
- Social relationships
- Education
- Character development
- Spiritual growth

They admitted to one another that neither of them was approaching discipline successfully. Johnny needed more structure than Maria had given him and more tenderness than he had received from his father.

Angelo and Maria discovered as they prayed and worked together on Johnny's behalf that they gained a new companionship they had been missing in their marriage. At last they were working in partnership with God and one another in one of the most important functions of any family—discipleship of a child.

Check the appendix/packet for materials your family can use in this daily task.

CHAPTER TEN

SHOW ME HOW TO LIVE

Linda stepped off the school bus, waved good-bye to her friend Sue, and walked slowly toward her house. Across the street she could see Rocker and Salvo watching her every move. Although she was only thirteen, she knew that her maturing body in low-buttoned blouses and tight pre-washed jeans was attracting the attention of boys much older than herself.

Their interest gave her a momentary high, but when she reached for her key and opened the door a familiar feeling of emptiness swept across her. No one was home. No one was ever home. When she was in kindergarten, her mother had always been there to greet her, but after that it was day care and then self care. She told everyone how much freedom she had, but she never said anything about the hurt. Before long, it would propel Linda on the road to tragedy.

Linda's parents were friendly and well-liked in their community. They were involved in a number of church and civic activities that took them out several nights a week after work. Linda always seemed to have something else to do, so they didn't mind leaving her after hastily prepared suppers night after night.

Although her parents didn't realize it, Linda needed their love and guidance even more as an adolescent than ever before. She was still basically at Motivational Level 2 and responded to approval, including that of her parents. Since they gave her little input, she turned almost exclusively to her peers. Most of her friends were also latch-key children who arrived home to empty houses and freedom to come and go as they pleased. Without their parents' approval or support, they got together and sought out a fast crowd of boys; they began dressing down to please them.

When Linda's grades began to drop, her parents reacted by grounding her for several weeks and insisting that she change her clothing and lifestyle. It didn't work. The punishment was too severe and too impersonal. Her parents never altered their full activity schedule nor took time to find out what was really going on in her life.

For a time, Linda appeared compliant, but with so little supervision she was able to sneak out with the same friends as before. When her parents were home, she would leave the house dressed the way they demanded, then change her clothes at a friend's house.

As her grades continued to drop, her parents finally realized that they would have to become more involved. They decided to move her to a different school where she would have a new peer group. Although they verbally expressed love and concern for their daughter and promised to curtail some of their activities, at no time did they seriously involve Linda in the changes they made in her life. Finally, she ran away.

Unknown to her parents, Linda had begun taking drugs. Fleeing to New York, she turned to prostitution to pay for her habit. For the next six months she sank further into depravity. Finally, in a rundown tenement, Linda was found dead.

What Teenagers Need

Linda's story is an extreme example of what can occur when parents lose touch with their children. It is meant not to frighten but to alert, to sound an alarm. Similar stories are occurring all over America today as more and more children experience teenage rebellion in a vacuum. With no parental structure to restrain this stage of growth, rebellion explodes into an overgrowth that dominates their lives. To the government, these children may be faceless statistics. To grieving families, they are tragic reminders of shattered dreams.

Discipleship of teenagers is different from that of younger children. When children reach adolescence, they are not only undergoing physical changes that will prepare them for adulthood but also undergoing spiritual and emotional changes that will chart the course of their future. Young children are taught to obey at home and school. Older children are equipped and sent out into the world.

Parents have no justification for abandoning discipleship when their children become teenagers. Those who take early retirement from parenting will live to regret it. Teenagers need someone to show them how to live. If they have no parents around to do it, they will find someone else. It is as simple as that.

It may be easy to say what teenagers need and who should give it to them, but it is a lot more complicated to understand how it can be done.

When the Apostle Paul was discipling a young preacher named Timothy, he gave him sound advice for leading his church that is also a powerful guide for parents leading their families. He told Timothy that the key to success in discipleship of the flock was to build it on the foundation of Scripture. This is what Paul wrote:

All Scripture is God-breathed and is useful for teaching, rebuking, correcting and training in righteousness, so that the man of God may be thoroughly equipped for every good work (2 Tim. 3:16-17 NIV).

The element of discipleship that involves teaching is the impartation of knowledge. To be a disciple is to be a learner. Parents in the role of teachers provide their young people with a knowledge of scriptural principles, the skills needed for everyday living, and insight gained over a lifetime of experience.

Rebuking and correcting are necessary because all of us are sinners. In love, God rebukes and corrects His children all their lives (Heb. 12:6), so children cannot expect to escape their parents' chastening just because their age is written in double digits.

To rebuke is to tell someone, "You did something wrong," and to correct is to say, "You should have done it this way." Parents who do nothing but rebuke their children are not providing them with positive alternatives. Those who give only correction are not communicating that they have broken absolute standards and are therefore sinners. Parents who practice both rebuke and correction have an orderly home and happier children who know their limits and don't have the constant tension of uncertain punishment. They are also preparing their children to accept the chastening and instruction of the Lord.

As children mature and increase in knowledge, they have a greater responsibility to live in conformity with God's laws. It is natural for them to rebel against parents and society, but they need someone to restrain that rebellion so they can find the way to the good life that God has prepared for them.

Because parents have experienced the blessings of

their own obedience, God has assigned them another task on behalf of their children: training in righteousness. Just as a gardener trains a vine on a trellis, so a parent trains his growing child to follow God's plan for his life. Young people want to go wild. They need parents there to consistently and gently direct them in the way they should go. If the Apostle Paul considered it important for a pastor to teach, rebuke, correct, and train his people in righteousness, how much more important it is for the parent to do this for the child.

Discipleship of teenagers fails most often because of two extremes: too much control or too little attention. Linda's parents thought that when she became a teenager their main responsibility for discipleship was ended. She didn't need their constant presence in her life to meet her basic needs of food and safety, so they assumed she didn't need them for much else either. That was their first mistake. Then, when she fell down because of their neglect, they imposed controls that were so unyielding that the tender vine of her life had no room to grow. Anger and rebellion were the fruit. Control without loving discipleship caused her to lose heart (Col. 3:21). When discipline continues at these extremes, unless God intervenes, the battle has already been lost.

When healthy discipling takes place, children develop good fruit naturally because through their parents' love, instruction, and prayers, the Holy Spirit begins to work inside of them. They begin to exhibit love, joy, peace, patience, kindness, goodness, gentleness, faithfulness, and self-control (Gal. 5:22,23).

Four Elements of Teenage Discipleship

Let's look at the four elements of discipleship from Paul's letter to Timothy: teaching, rebuking, correcting, and training in righteousness.

TEACHING

In every generation, too many children learn what is acceptable behavior by being punished for doing what is wrong instead of being taught by proper instruction what is right. Paul wrote to parents about a different way. He said, "Provoke not your children to wrath: but bring them up in the nurture and admonition of the Lord" (Eph. 6:4 KJV). Godly instruction is positive. It allows parents to present what they would like to see happen in their children's lives and then work with them to accomplish it.

Moses said (Deut. 6:1-9) that teaching of children should take place when you sit at home or walk on the road, when you lie down and when you get up. It should be as prominent as the very door frames of the house. Teenagers are hard to pin down to a time of family devotions, but if teaching is as important as the Bible says, parents should be as flexible as necessary to see that it gets done. In the teen years, much teaching may be informal, such as sympathy during a girlfriend/boyfriend crisis, support during conflict with a sex education teacher, searching for answers when a friend gets in trouble with drugs. There is no required environmental setting for learning about God's ways.

Teaching should include principles—bedrock concepts from the Bible that are necessary for success in life. Some teenagers, especially those who have experienced trials, think God doesn't love them and are afraid to give Him control of their lives. They have a sense of sin and will make professions of faith, but they find it difficult to be consistent Christians. Parents can help by:

- Helping them set long- and short-range goals (See appendix/packet for a contract your child can use for setting improved behavior goals.)
- Teaching about Bible characters who found it difficult to be disciples
- Allowing them to take a few tumbles
- Loving and forgiving them every time they backslide

- Reminding them that their own strength will never be sufficient to help them be righteous
- Tuning them in to the power of God
- Speaking often of the joy that comes with obedience

REBUKING AND CORRECTING

It is usually easier to rebuke and correct a younger child than an older one. Older ones don't feel obligated to accept a parent's ruling that "You'll do this because I say so." Teenagers force their parents to come up with reasons. This may seem like a nuisance at first and a loss of control, but although it can be abused, at its best it is an integral part of training these young people to be parents themselves. They are capable of understanding a great deal more at this stage about right and wrong and need to build their own internal assurance that there is a higher law than parental force.

It is important to dialogue with Level 3 and 4 children on a more mature level than younger ones. The same strategies for winning compliance simply won't work. Although parents must never abdicate their position and become undemanding buddies, if young people are treated like adults they will begin to act like them.

Parents of teenagers need to be careful not to judge the hearts of their children. That is the responsibility of God. Some behavior may seem to indicate a certain motive or condition of the heart, but the behavior itself should be dealt with, not speculations about why the child has done it.

When a teenager launches a verbal barrage at his parents, he should be rebuked and corrected. He should be told that this is not acceptable behavior, and future conversations must demonstrate respect and restraint. The parents don't have to explain themselves or assume he has had a bad day. They can appeal to the principle taught in the Fifth Commandment: "Honor your father and your mother, so that you may live long in the land the Lord your God is giving you" (Ex. 20:12 NIV). That doesn't make parents hard-hearted. Certain rules need to be enforced continually for the good of all concerned.

Rebuking and correcting will inevitably be carried out differently by those with different personalities:

Ruler parents must be very careful with teenagers, because their domineering style will drive young people to rebellion. These parents must make an effort to give children at this level an opportunity to participate.

Designer parents carefully spend time on instruction, but sometimes they neglect the personal interaction their teenagers need. With a conscious effort to be demonstrative, they can provide their children with a strong sense of stability in their teen years.

Promoter parents want to be liked by everyone. That causes two problems with teenagers: They have difficulty enforcing rules, and they tend to put up a front with the public. When they correct these problems, they are able to earn the respect of their children and are greatly loved.

Teenagers love to talk to Server parents because they are such good listeners, but they are too willing to bend family rules. With God's help, they can gain the discernment and firmness they need to hold their teenagers accountable and still love them.

Rebuke and correction are essential, even at this age, because young people are still very definitely in the formative stage. They are often determined to swim against the current their parents have set in motion. They need disagreeable consequences of their misbehavior that are enforced. However, they should not be so demoralized with punishment that they lose all desire to be good. The goal is to get them to go with the flow of life as God has established it.

Training in Righteousness

If most adolescents were asked what goal they wanted to accomplish when they turned sixteen, they would probably place high on the list "Getting a driver's license." They won't be able to get it, however, if all they do is read textbooks, study the law, listen to class lectures, or sit next to instructors who do the driving. They won't learn how to drive themselves until they actually get behind the wheel. In the same way, children need real life experiences in discerning right from wrong to help them grow to maturity. It is up to parents to provide them.

Training in righteousness is not something harsh or confining. It is something that shows young people how to find the blessing of God because "The fruit of the righteous is a tree of life" (Prov. 11:30 NIV).

These are some of the areas that will benefit from daily training and will help prepare the child for adulthood:

- Respect for parents
- Participation in household tasks
- Obedience to house rules and acceptance of penalties
- Developing a Christian life
- Devotional life
- Self-control
- Morality
- Love and encouragement toward family members
- Leadership training

In your appendix/packet is a Discipline Plan to help your Level 3 or 4 child take greater responsibility for his behavior and growth. It includes the following questions: "What did I do? What rule did I break? Why was it a problem? What is my plan to solve the problem or avoid the situation next time?" It also contains instructions on how to use it.

When parents require that their children give them respect and honor, they are not only meeting their own need for a pleasant home environment but also enforcing God's commandment in order to open a door of blessing.

Notice this contrast between Level 3 and Level 1 obedience:

Dad could say to his Level 3 child, "Todd, I'm running late. Could you take the trash out before you go to school? Today is pick-up day." Todd would probably respond, "Sure," and then follow through.

If he were talking to his Level 1 child, Dad would be more directive: "Cheryl, I can't take the trash out because I'm late. You have another twenty minutes before you go to school. Please be sure you take the barrels out or we will be stuck with smelly garbage for another week."

If Cheryl whined, "But Dad, "I'm still fixing my hair. I won't have time," Dad might have to add, "You've been fixing your hair for twenty minutes. You can finish up in ten minutes—fifteen at the latest. I expect you to take the trash out to the street, O.K.?"

If Cheryl still complains, Dad will have to revert to an even more directive style: "Cheryl, this garbage needs to get to the street, and I expect you to do it. I will be very upset if I come home and you haven't done what I have asked. Is that clear?"

When children slip in their motivational level, it is best to become temporarily more directive and also to determine what is causing them to backslide. Be sure that you don't slip into condemnation, however. Confront in love, be patient, and adjust your style to match their level. Then begin again.

Any further resistance by Cheryl would amount to open rebellion. When Dad got home, he would need to pull her aside and talk about her attitude and the need to obey her parents, imposing whatever penalty has been agreed upon in the past. He will give her rules to guide her responses in the future, along with consequences if the rules are not followed. And all of this will be done with love and respect.

The next time Dad asks something of a similar nature and Cheryl complies, he should take time to praise her cooperation. He might even say, "Hey, I appreciate the way you responded this morning when I needed help. Why don't we grab a burger at McDonald's so that Mom doesn't have to cook dinner?"

This gives Cheryl encouragement and tangible rewards that can help her grow. (Notice that he didn't use the outing as a bribe but as a natural consequence of family cooperation.) As Cheryl matured, he would reward her materially on a less consistent basis, but by this time she would be moving into Level 2, and simple praise would often be sufficient as a reinforcer.

Parents themselves are responsible for doing their part to earn their children's respect. At this age, young people are especially conscious of inconsistencies in their parents. As they await their own parenthood experience, they are absorbing every act of their parents as a model for the years to come. If parents want deep, lasting respect, they must walk closely with the Lord and live a life of integrity. They must be honest with their children, admitting their own failures and asking forgiveness when they have acted unjustly. Parents also need to be honest enough to tell their children when they are hurt deeply by their behavior. Strong communication skills that are built during the teen years will be invaluable in their work, church, marriage, and family relationships of the future.

Teenagers are preparing for independence, but with that freedom come added responsibilities. They will always have their share of household tasks, so chores should be a part of any discipleship process. Children should be assigned tasks according to their level of ability and given praise and rewards appropriate to age and motivational level. Parents should expect their young people to take on an increasing number of responsibilities without being told.

The major rules of the house in any family should be short, clear, and positive. Penalties should be clearly defined and enforced quickly and consistently. Rules should be a vehicle for building relationships, not a means of establishing tyranny. One of the best ways to assure success is to invite the child's participation in making the rules that will govern his behavior. Respect his counsel and implement as many of his ideas as possible. Except in cases of immature, persistent rebellion, a parent needs to change from the authoritarian rule needed at Levels 1 and 2 to something more suitable to maturing teens.

Before your child is placed in any compromising situations, sit down together and talk about temptations that are likely to arise. As new problems come, help them work out ways to deal with them. Remind them at all times that "the Lord knows how to rescue the godly from temptation" (2 Peter 2:9 NASB). Show them that although their friends say they have freedom in their wild lifestyles, they are actually enslaved to their lusts (2 Pet. 2:19).

Leadership Training

Training in righteousness equips children from Christian homes to be leaders in every field. Parents can train future leaders—or even strong, stable followers—if they follow these guidelines:

Be available. Don't make your children resort to destructive methods to get your attention.

Give them a chance to take risks. Allow them increasing levels of freedom and flexibility so they can develop competence. Remember that "the letter [of the law] kills, but the Spirit gives life" (2 Cor. 3:6 NIV).

Show them the difference between healthy risks and unhealthy ones. "The prudent sees the evil and hides himself, but the naive go on, and are punished for it" (Prov. 22:3 NASB).

Continue to require righteous behavior. Impose appropriate penalties as necessary. Remind them that they can take control of their lives and will find the power they need in the Holy Spirit.

Don't continually rescue your children from the natural consequences of their actions. "A short-tempered man must bear his own penalty; you can't do much to help him. If you try once, you must try a dozen times! (Prov. 19:19 TLB).

Spend more time encouraging good behavior than you do correcting misbehavior. Build them up so they have confidence in their ability to achieve.

Watch for signs of discouragement or helplessness. Bring about restoration.

Be realistic about their strengths and weaknesses. Help them choose activities that are most suited to them.

Listen attentively day or night, whenever they want to talk to you. Teach them the skills of problem solving by walking through their crises with them.

Pray continually for patience and wisdom. Pray with them as often as they are willing. Remind them that God loves them too much to let them escape the penalty for their misdeeds, whether you are there to see them or not.

Parental Unity

Jeff and Cindy were the parents of a thirteen-year-old son named Cameron. In recent months Cameron had matured motivationally and shown a willingness to accept more responsibility, so they allowed him to go to a hockey game with his friends. However, when he arrived home after midnight, long past his 9:30 P.M. curfew, they were frantic and had even called the police.

When Cameron walked in the door, his parents were both relieved and angry. Cameron had trouble seeing what was wrong. There had been a surprise snowfall, so after the game he and the other boys had walked over to the big hill behind the school to go sledding. "I was with the guys," he said, looking with confusion from one to the other. "We watched out for each other."

Cindy told him, "You knew you were safe, but we didn't; and besides, you promised to be home by 9:30." Cameron was grounded for the next weekend and told that he couldn't go with the other boys to another hockey game unless a parent was present. "When we decide that you are able to handle the responsibility of coming home on time," Jeff said, "we'll consider letting you go alone."

Two weeks later Cameron asked, "Dad, can I go with

the guys over to watch the Lancers play hockey tonight?"

Jeff and Cindy had anticipated his request and talked about it when they were alone together, as was their practice. They knew that decisions made in the heat of the moment were often regretted later. After Cameron had broken his curfew, Jeff and Cindy had seen that, like a typical adolescent, he could demonstrate Level 2 or 3 behavior with them but with his peers act more like a Level 1 child. They used the controlling stategy of grounding, but were prepared to move him to a more supportive strategy of self-monitoring as soon as possible.

Thus, when Cameron spoke to him, Jeff said to his son, "What will be different this time?"

Cameron said quickly, "I'll be home when I'm supposed to!"

"What if you boys decide that there is something else that's real exciting to do after the game? How will you handle that?"

Cameron paused. "Well, if everybody wants to do something, it will be hard for me to just leave and go home. What if I call you and ask permission even though I know you won't let me? That way you can say 'No' for me."

Jeff said, "Okay, Cameron. I appreciate why you need a backup and I don't mind helping you out. Mom and I will let you go this time, but remember, under no circumstances will you be allowed out after 9:30. When you feel more comfortable standing up to the pressure, you'll be able to do it without my help, but for now I think you have a good solution."

After Cameron successfully handled the event, Jeff and Cindy sat down with him to "debrief," asking how he had handled the peer pressure and providing suggestions as necessary. They took time to compliment him on the way he accepted responsibility, giving him another incentive to strive for Level 3 behavior even with his friends.

When children at Level 2 approach adolescence, their desire for approval shifts from parents and other authority figures to their adolescent peer group. Wise parents, finding themselves in competition for the hearts and minds of their children, will not lose their influence if they continue to maintain reasonable structure and stay involved and interested in their child's activities. They will also say, "I will put a muzzle on my mouth" (Ps. 39:1 NIV), so they don't gossip about their children or embarrass them in front of others.

In the opening story, Linda's parents were oblivious to her needs. When they didn't give her enough attention and approval she sought it elsewhere, unfortunately from children who were still at Level 1. Ultimately she, too, slipped down to their level and became her own authority, eventually taking drugs and running away. She escaped the hastily inflicted controls of her parents only to find that her life without them had no controls at all.

Maturity at Level 4

When children begin functioning on Level 4 they are truly mature. Their primary goal is to be obedient to their parents and to serve God in any way He desires. All of us have the capability of functioning at Level 4 but few of us ever attain it consistently. At that level Christ, and not self, reigns in the heart. When you see your children demonstrating this kind of maturity, show them how to serve others by assuming leadership roles in the home, church, and community.

Contrasted with those at lower levels, children who function at Level 4 seem able to maintain their level of motivation even during times of stress. They need little external enforcement to make them behave properly or to complete a task. Whatever they do is unto God. They still appreciate others' encouragement, but that is not their main goal.

Even though these children can function at a mature level in some areas, don't give them tasks and responsibilities for which they are not developmentally, chronologically or emotionally prepared. Take time to listen and find out what they are thinking and feeling. Be aware of their physical, emotional, and spiritual condition.

Take into account their personality differences, which will become increasingly evident as they grow. Match your disciplinary actions and communication style to your child as an individual.

Punishment does not usually work well with children at this level. In situations where your child has erred, provide a face-saving escape by offering a choice such as, "The lawn should have been mowed by 3:00. You can either complete it now, or skip the movie and do it at 4:00." Your child is aware of his failure, but realizes that since it is unusual, you have provided him with a chance to redeem himself.

In many ways, Level 4 parenting is the easiest. Parents still have the responsibility to make certain ultimate decisions, but they can often achieve cooperation with their children at this level simply by describing a situation and inviting their help. Look in the appendix/packet for extra assistance.

The longer you wait, the harder it is to disciple your child, but it is never too late for God. Some of the greatest pastors and evangelists were converted to Christ as teenagers or even later. Sometimes it may seem that all you can do is trust God, love them, and feed them, but you can be sure that even if you don't think they heard you, God will keep an account. He will honor your work in His name, and will not let go of your child.

CHAPTER ELEVEN

PARENT-TEACHER RELATIONSHIPS

The first day of school! Tommy was excited. His big sister Terry loved school and had been playing games with him every day. Tommy ran off to school with joy. He returned home with gloom.

"What happened?" asked Tommy's father, Richard, as they played croquet after supper. Tommy was noncommittal. "What's your new teacher like?" he asked.

"She's bossy," Tommy said immediately. "She yells at kids for nothing. I'm gonna make sure she never gets mad at me."

"Once you get to know her I'm sure you'll find she's a nice person," said Richard.

In the days and weeks that followed, Tommy said little about school and he told his sister, "I hate school! I'm never going to play it any more."

Tommy's first grade report was a shocker. It read "Excellent" in conduct and "N" for "Needs Improvement" or "U" for "Unsatisfactory" in every other category. Richard and his wife Cheryl were stunned. Tommy was unable to talk about it. Richard called the school office the next day and set up an appointment to meet Tommy's teacher.

Mrs. Iverson greeted them warmly saying, "I expected to hear from you when I sent Tommy's papers home at mid-term."

"We didn't receive any papers from Tommy," Cheryl said uneasily.

"I take it he hasn't been talking to you about his problems?" she asked.

"No," Richard answered. "He hardly talks about school."

Mrs. Iverson said, "When Tommy started school I tried to help him grasp the material, but he was unresponsive. Sometimes he seemed quite fearful. Have you ever thought about putting him in counseling?"

Richard battled the anger welling up inside of him. Controlling his voice he said, "Something happened to Tommy the first day of school. He was excited about it in the morning but that night he seemed sad and disappointed. He said the teacher yelled at the kids and he was going to make sure she never yelled at him."

Mrs. Iverson was listening carefully. "I know I'm a direct person who runs a tight, no-nonsense classroom," she said, "but I'm surprised he thought I was yelling. That isn't my style."

Cheryl said, "Tommy is a gentle boy. He pulls back when someone is too assertive. This time I think it kept him from learning from you. You probably just spoke firmly. He translated that into yelling because he doesn't hear that approach at home."

"Apparently his fear of me has made it impossible for him to learn," Mrs. Iverson said. "We can't let that continue. How can we work this out together?"

Richard and Cheryl gratefully arranged for Mrs. Iverson to stop by their house to meet Tommy in a less stressful environment, and in the weeks to come they worked as a team to help Tommy learn.

Dynamics of Parent-Teacher Interaction

Tommy's situation was resolved for several reasons. The parents, although they should have investigated the situation sooner, did some things right. They:

- Knew their child's personality
- Knew their child's needs
- Took the responsibility to get his needs met
- Were not intimidated by the teacher
- Saw the teacher as their assistant
- Respected the teacher
- Knew that they were qualified to evaluate their own child

The teacher was helpful because she:

- Was at a high motivational level
- Was willing to listen to the parents
- Considered the parents to be experts on their child
- Was aware of her personality style
- Understood how her style affected others
- Was willing to make adjustments to help her pupil and his parents
- Took time to get to know her student personally

Unfortunately, many children who have personality conflicts with their teachers don't have parents or teachers who know how to remedy the situation. In this chapter, we will show you how to use the knowledge you have acquired thus far in the book to work with teachers and successfully improve your child's school performance.

Parents who have children in any school— public or private— have a clear biblical mandate to take responsibility for their children's education. They may temporarily delegate the task of educating their children to a teacher, Christian or non-Christian, but they never relinquish jurisdiction.

What happens in school classrooms eventually affects all of society. Parents can provide valuable oversight to this powerful institution. Abraham Lincoln expressed it well when he said, "The philosophy of the classroom today is the practice of government tomorrow."

Winning the Partnership of the Teacher

Parents and teachers have become increasingly distant from one another. In the days before American society became so mobile, teachers might see two generations of children pass through their classrooms, because they all lived together in the same community. However, the mobility of the population, the consolidation of school districts, and the breakdown between community and church life have made the nation increasingly faceless.

If parents become involved in their children's schools, they can reestablish the partnerships they once had with teachers. They can treat teachers not as enemies but as friends and co-laborers. The impersonal schools cannot be expected to cure all America's problems. They are not equipped for such a task. They need to work with parents.

Teachers do not know as much about their students as their parents do. They may know more about certain subjects in the curriculum, but parents know better than anyone else their children's personalities, methods of communication, and expressions of deep feelings. They know what conditions have to be present for their children to learn effectively, what words encourage them, and which discourage them. Unless the teacher knows not only what is being taught but also who is being taught, she will never be effective. Only the parent can provide that perspective.

At the beginning of the school year, parents need to meet with their child's teacher to establish a cooperative relationship. At that time, they will be able to discover if the teacher is willing to work with them or not. If there is obviously no hope for cooperation, they should insist on a different teacher.

If parents wait until the first grading period or until the teacher has called for a conference, as Tommy's parents did, the tone will be set. If the first few weeks have been unsuccessful, the only way the teacher can think differently about the child is to rescript her mind. However, if her first contact with the child is preceded by a parental briefing, she will have a head start on giving him the best educational experience possible.

When parents call for a conference, some teachers will become aloof or defensive. They will make comments like, "I've been teaching for five years now, and I know how to do my job." They may even say, "I have a very successful style of teaching. If your child will comply with my requests, I can guarantee he will be successful." Both statements reflect a low level of maturity on the part of the teacher. The teacher in the first statement is acting defensively; the second is saying that one style of teaching is best for everyone, regardless of individual needs.

These attitudes are counterproductive to a healthy parent-teacher relationship and harmful to the child. You cannot afford to have your child influenced by a teacher who considers you incompetent or interfering. Your child may be able to learn effectively from a teacher who differs from your ideal in some respects, but if there is no cooperation, you must take action. God gave you the responsibility for those children, and He expects you to get them the best care and instruction possible. Don't settle for peace at any cost. Do whatever is necessary to fulfill your commitment to God.

Personality Differences in Teachers

Each teacher has a personality style and level of motivation that determines how she relates to parents and to the children in her class. In the opening story, Tommy's teacher operated at a high motivational level and was not threatened by the parents' concerns. She understood her tendency to be domineering and was willing to adapt to a sensitive little boy.

Parents need to have at least a general idea of the teacher's motivational level and personality so they can predict where their child and the teacher will clash and where they should be successful.

When a teacher is operating at a low level of motivation, it may not be obvious until she is observed in a stressful situation or asked to make changes in her style of teaching.

The only way to discover the teacher's personality style and level of motivation is to get to know her. That is why we recommend you make that visit to the teacher. Observe her reactions as you share information about your child. The following descriptions will help you identify the teacher's motivational level and personality style. Not all of these characteristics will be appropriate, but they will help you draw general conclusions.

CHARACTERISTICS OF THE LEVEL 1 TEACHER

Self-centered. The classroom seems to be run for the teacher's convenience rather than for the children.

Set in her ways. Rarely exceeds basic expectations unless she anticipates a reward.

Defensive. Personalizes comments and may get angry.

Critical of authority. Complains about superiors.

EFFECTIVE APPROACHES TO THE LEVEL 1 TEACHER

Be direct and specific when talking to teachers at this level. Avoid confrontation, but let the teacher know exactly where you stand. Make an extra effort to be friendly. Be sure to affirm her by stressing the importance of her role in your child's life. Frequent interactions with these teachers are helpful and will insure adherence to the matters you have discussed.

CHARACTERISTICS OF THE LEVEL 2 TEACHER

Seeks your approval. Paints a positive picture of herself.

Sensitive. Feelings may be easily hurt if everything you say is not definitely positive.

Eager to please. Will give the impression that she is trying hard to please you.

Blaming authorities. Instead of expressing her own convictions, she may invoke the name of a supervisor to explain why she can't or won't do what you ask.

EFFECTIVE APPROACHES TO THE LEVEL 2 TEACHER

Be direct and specific with this teacher but at the same time be gentle. This teacher desires your approval and will work hard to achieve it, particularly if you maintain regular contact. Make sure the affirmation you show is personally directed to her. Frequently tell her how much you appreciate her efforts.

CHARACTERISTICS OF THE LEVEL 3 TEACHER

Businesslike. Demonstrates a knowledge and understanding of the issues involved.

Seeks approval indirectly. Wins your favor by demonstrating specific ability to solve a problem.

Analytical. Carefully weighs information in order to be fair.

Follows the rules. Adheres carefully to formal rules and regulations.

EFFECTIVE APPROACHES TO THE LEVEL 3 TEACHER

Ask this teacher for her suggestions on how to best achieve your goals for your child. Enter into the discussion with your own ideas. Your approach should be collegial, two people with a common interest in helping your child. Affirm her more in terms of outcomes and goals that she has already met rather than making simple statements that you appreciate her as a person. This is important, but no longer takes priority. A Level 3 teacher will need less contact from you to follow up on your suggestions.

CHARACTERISTICS OF THE LEVEL 4 TEACHER

Honorable. Wants to do what is right and is able to balance concerns of people with those of the institution.

Thorough. Will consider all angles and try to choose the best course.

Generous. Will demonstrate self-sacrifice and a willingness to go the extra mile.

Humble. Does not seek comments that would be the least self-serving.

Committed. Frequently demonstrates devotion to her profession.

EFFECTIVE APPROACHES TO THE LEVEL 4 TEACHER

This teacher will take the initiative to call you whenever possible. Since she will not always have the time, however, make occasional contacts to check on how things are going. You need not be looking over this teacher's shoulder. This teacher is your partner. She is not dependent on your praise in order to do her job well, but she does appreciate it. Be pervasive in the love you show her.

Effects of Personality on Teaching Style

Teachers tend to create classroom environments according to their motivational levels and personalities. If they are aware of the way their style differs from that of their students, they can make the necessary adjustments. However, if they are unaware of differences or unwilling to adapt, they can do great damage, especially in the early primary years when children are still in the formative stages of learning.

If young children are unable to learn from a particular teacher, they may carry with them a feeling of failure for the rest of their school years. That is why it is so important for parents to understand their children and find out about their teachers. If the child becomes frustrated by the educational process, he may become rebellious, apathetic, or overly submissive (like Tommy at the beginning of the chapter), or plead sickness frequently so he can avoid school. The child blessed with an adaptable teacher will continually show improvement, because his learning style is matched with a complementary teaching style.

You already know your child's personality style. Here are some clues to identify the teacher's personality style. Remember that when a teacher is at a low level of motivation, her personality style must complement that of the child or problems will arise. Refer to chapter four again to see which sending styles provoke the best responses from each individual. Teachers at higher levels will be willing and able to adapt to the needs of almost any child.

RULER TEACHER
- Takes charge of parent meeting almost immediately
- Gets to the point quickly
- Talks about results
- Emphasizes academics more than personalities, analysis more than feelings
- Often projects a controlled demeanor
- Is quick to challenge when disagrees
- Weighs your ideas about your child rather than accepting them at face value
- Maintains eye contact, particularly when making a point

DESIGNER TEACHER
- Seems to be an organized, conscientious person
- Is helpful but probably does not exude friendliness

- Listens carefully to what you say and asks for details
- Tends to be diplomatic and analytical, but may reserve judgment on the truth of your assertions
- Can lay out specifically what she intends to teach and how she will go about it
- May adhere strictly to the school system's expectations as her standard for performance
- Is clear and methodical
- Does not appear assertive but will make sure you understand her point
- May break off eye contact when discussing ideas

PROMOTER TEACHER
- Greets you quickly and sociably
- Is expressive when talking, using hand gestures
- Seems fired up about the coming year
- Is interested in your personal description of your child
- May be articulate in an upbeat way
- Focuses on feelings more than details
- Maintains eye contact in a friendly way
- Is willing to keep in touch with you

SERVER TEACHER
- Greets you warmly and makes sure you are comfortable
- Gives the impression of being relaxed and laid back
- Doesn't interrupt you but waits patiently to hear you out
- Appears to have an even disposition
- Is interested in your feelings
- Can describe to you what subjects will be emphasized
- Refers to products and feelings more than specific tasks
- Avoids eye contact when conflicts arise

As you will recall, each personality style has its own method of sending and receiving messages. A teacher sends messages all day long and her style of teaching is greatly affected by her personality. Once you identify her personality style, reread chapter four to see how she will communicate with your child and how you can best communicate with her.

How Children Learn

Current research indicates clearly that not all children learn in the same way. You know from previous chapters that at any given time your child is at a certain motivational level (varying from self-centered to self-sacrificing), is exercising certain gifts, and looks at life from the perspective of his personality style. Because of these differences, certain methods of learning are more effective for one group than another. Servers, for example, thrive on drills and could probably do a set every day. Rulers don't like workbook education. They prefer fast-paced discussions and independent projects— activities that can be threatening to Servers.

Children can develop serious learning problems when teachers fail to consider these natural inclinations. Before you allow your child to be labeled "learning disabled," search all avenues to make sure his teachers have been matching their teaching styles to your child's needs. He may be capable of learning a great deal, but no one has ever figured out his style.

Children's learning patterns are affected not only by internal factors but also by the classroom environment, distractions from other children, the mood of the teacher, and their own moods and emotional problems. They are affected by hunger, fatigue, love, and hate. Some will become incorrigible when they are simply bored. Learning is an extremely complex process influenced by many factors, not simply by intelligence.

As you observe your child at home, you will see him at his best and at his worst. You will discover signs the teacher can watch for that will make her job much easier. You already know the motivational levels of your children. If you look at the following description, you will know how to best teach them at home, as part of the natural course of family life, and how they will best learn at school. Later you can pass on this information to the teacher. You will also find it invaluable for teaching your child at home. Whether or not you are a "home-schooler," you are your child's primary teacher.

LEVEL 1 LEARNERS

These children will lose their sense of security unless they have a consistently structured environment with clearly defined rules and immediate rewards. When new material is introduced, it should be given in small doses with lots of personal attention. If they seem to withdraw or become overly aggressive, they are probably expressing insecurity about their schoolwork or environment. When they misbehave, since they are primarily self-centered, they will often try to blame others, even if they have to lie. Stories read aloud are very effective. Display of their work is a great encouragement, and classroom chores give them a sense of responsibility.

LEVEL 2 LEARNERS

These children seek recognition from their friends, sometimes with methods inappropriate for the classroom. Daily goals, rules, and incentives for treating their classmates with kindness are helpful at this stage. These children should be given opportunities to make choices and then held accountable for their decisions. They still need rewards for their activities and respond well to praise from a teacher they admire.

LEVEL 3 LEARNERS

Because they are beginning to work more coopera-
tively with others, these children desire to be respected for
their behavior, although they can still be driven to lower
levels when treated poorly. Level 3 learners exhibit more
perseverance and diligence than less mature children and
are willing to encourage others in the classroom to express
themselves. It is wise to give these children a role in setting
standards for the classroom.

LEVEL 4 LEARNERS

Teachers find these students a joy. They are persistent
and eager learners, even when presented with difficult
circumstances. The teacher should give them more freedom
from structure so that they can act on their own initiative
and learn to follow through on commitments to others.

How Personality Style Affects Learning

As you will recall from chapter four, personality style
influences the way an individual tends to react when someone sends a communication his way. These responses are
the person's listening and learning styles. The following
descriptions apply this information on communication and
personalities to the classroom situation.

RULER STUDENTS

Rulers are such independent learners that they
sometimes resent being told pat answers and expected to
accept them. Lectures don't reach a Ruler if they are
standard, straightforward talks. Rulers need more interesting presentations if they are to remain attentive. They are
fascinated by the way things work.

Demonstrations are not well received by Rulers unless they are short, relevant attention-getters. Discussions
are effective if fast-paced and open-ended. The teacher
should be aware that Rulers may try to dominate the group
and will need kind but firm reminders to yield the floor.

The most effective way to teach Rulers is to give them assignments that allow them to construct something or plan and carry out a project. Exercises are also effective, but teachers must not use too many workbooks, written question/answer formats, or long-term commitments because it stifles their independent thinking. Rulers are not good candidates for programmed learning.

Designer Students

Designers are introspective learners, processing information in their minds and constructing their own portrait of reality. They can learn from lectures and demonstrations if the presentations are coherent and non-repetitive. They like to take notes and will listen for long periods of time if the lecture makes sense to them. Large group discussions are not effective with Designers, but they like small groups where they can debate and solve problems together. They enjoy mastering the use of logic.

When assignments are given, the Designer must have facts and information readily available for studying the problem so they can develop and apply theories. Designers are willing to undertake long-term projects that allow them to invent, discover, and design. Use exercises for Designers if they involve problem-solving and decision-making.

In all their work, Designers will usually strive for high grades and honors.

Promoter Students

Promoters are restless in a classroom because they find the confinement, routine, and detailed paperwork to be stressful. Lectures and demonstrations are effective methods for teaching Promoters if the presentations are lively and there is plenty of human interest.

Promoters like to hear stories and remember them well. If they are to learn technical details, they must be given plenty of repetition. Discussions are popular with Promoters, especially if given in small groups with opportunity for interaction. They enjoy assignments if they are allowed to be creative and expressive (e.g., writing a drama, recording a play or story). Promoters are constant sources of new ideas. Exercises are effective and may involve competition with others, although Promoters especially like cooperative efforts. They enjoy poetry and other media they can use to communicate what is important to them.

SERVER STUDENTS

Lectures and demonstrations are effective for Servers if they are about people and their feelings, follow an outline, and are well organized and clearly presented. Repetition is desired and welcomed. If Servers are to be involved in discussions, give them notice in advance so they can be prepared. In general, they would rather be spectators than participants, reflecting on what they see and feel.

Assignments are very effective for Servers, especially if they include drill and clerical tasks such as workbooks and programmed learning materials, but Servers will not thrive if forced to work alone for extended periods of time. When they are unhappy with their learning experience, they lose self-confidence, becoming moody, resentful, and withdrawn.

Exercises are ineffective for Servers if they require spontaneity and inventiveness. Servers like the security of structure. They will gladly memorize information and answer questions on it. They also like to figure things out using step-by-step thinking processes. Good instruction teaches them how to do that, and answers for them the question, "Why do I have to learn this?"

Helping with Homework

Although homework was once reserved for children in seventh grade or above, it is increasingly being given during the primary years. Parents often struggle with how much to help their children with their homework and how to avoid starting a battle of tempers or ending up doing the work themselves. Here is an example of how one family handled it.

Matthew was a Promoter child in the fifth grade who usually operated at Level 3. His father, Stu, was a Designer and his mother, Mary, a Server. Stu and Mary knew from past experience that Matthew needed time with them after dinner just to be friends before he could effectively launch into his homework. Matthew loved to laugh and would probably talk and laugh himself through the entire homework hour if he had his way.

One evening, Matthew was particularly full of enthusiastic stories about school. Mary knew it was important to let him share his enthusiasm for a while, so she sat down and listened attentively to his exploits before requiring him to get to work. After a while she told him, "It's been fun hearing about your day, but now it's time to get to work." Then they prayed together that God would clear his mind and help him understand his homework.

That night Matthew had a harder time than usual settling down. By prearranged agreement, at this point Mary, with her gentle Server style, yielded to Stu, with his orderly Designer style.

"What's the first assignment on your list?" asked Stu.

Matthew answered, "Math, pages 43 and 44. Dad, do you know what happened in spelling today?"

Stu answered, "I heard you telling Mom about it. Congratulations on winning the spelling bee. I always told you that you were a good speller because you studied your words. You have some studying to do in math now so you can be good at that, too."

"O.K., Dad," said Matthew with a grin, "I catch your drift."

As Matthew opened his book, Stu said, "I have to use the phone now, so ask Mom if you need any help. One of us needs to check your work before you pack up. O.K.?"

"O.K., Dad."

After a few quiet moments, Matthew said, "Mom, I'm stuck."

Mary came in from the other room and picked up his homework paper. "Let's see, you're doing long division," she said. What are the steps you need to do first?"

"I forget."

"Look at the example in the book," Mary said. "What are the steps?"

Matthew said, "Step 1 is . . ." and rattled off the steps.

"That's right," Mary said. "Now show me how you did Step 1 with this problem." Matthew proceeded to show her Steps 2, 3, and 4 until he realized that his problem had arisen with Step 4. Mary saw his mistake before he did, but she waited patiently for him to discover it.

"I see what I need to do now," Matthew said. "Thanks, Mom." With a hand companionably resting on his shoulder, Mary waited briefly to be sure he was settled in on the right course.

By the time Matthew was finished, Stu was ready to take over again.

"Dad, I'm done," Matthew said.

Stu entered the room and matched the completed assignments with the teacher's list. Matthew was not insulted by this checking, because it was part of the family routine. He knew that his parents had helped him in the past when he almost missed some work that would have cost him the next day at school.

"I think you're ready for tomorrow," Stu said. "You'll do a good job now that you know the material. Maybe your teacher will let you help some of your friends in the class if they couldn't figure it out." The night's work done, Matthew went off happily to play with his friends.

Let's analyze some of the successful methods used by Stu and Mary to help their son with his homework.

Provide structure with love. Mary took time to meet Matthew's need to visit briefly before she expected him to get to work. Stu didn't neglect the opportunity to give praise to his son before he guided him back to his studies.

Bring God into the picture. Except for Christian schools, mention of God has been banned from the classroom. In the home, parents are free to remind their children of the truth that God is always there to guide them.

Encourage independent study. Stu left the room after his son was back on track. At Level 3 Matthew could work independently and didn't need his father to guide him through every step. Children at lower motivational levels need more frequent supervision by parents but should still be steered toward the goal of more independent study.

Use the best communication style for the task. Before Mary responded to Matthew's call for help, she knew she could be most helpful to him at this point if she assumed the communication style of a Designer, like her husband. Matthew needed structure more than a friendly chat.

Use patience and restraint. With a few words Mary helped Matthew discover for himself why he was stuck. Then she patiently led him to an appropriate solution.

Refer the child to reference books. Children won't always have their parents around to help them find the answers. They need to be reminded to make use of their textbooks and other resources.

Give praise for a job well done. Parents can have a strong positive effect on their children's attitudes toward studying by taking a moment to praise them each time they accomplish a goal.

Remind them of ways to serve others. Stu knew that at Level 3 children are more highly motivated when they find ways to win respect from others by passing on their expertise. This need was heightened in Matthew because he was a Promoter and loved encouraging others to do bigger and better things.

Preparing to Meet with the Teacher

In your appendix/packet are materials to help you make a presentation to your child's teacher. Much of this information will be drawn from exercises you did in previous chapters—your child's motivational level, gifts, personality, communication style, etc.—as well as the subjects covered in the current chapter.

Before you visit with the teacher, you and your spouse need more than information, however. You also need to understand your right to call that meeting. You need to be secure in the knowledge that God has given you jurisdiction over your child's education. For this reason, the first exercise in the packet will take you through Scripture verses that give you that assurance. You will be able to see how God exhorts parents to love their children and to teach them according to His ways.

Meeting with the teacher should open up a dialogue that proves extremely valuable for your child's growth. Try not to overwhelm the teacher with all the information you have compiled. Talk about only those items that are most critical, then leave the rest of the information with her so she can look it over at her leisure. Set up another meeting a short time later to discuss your child's early progress and verify that the teacher has read your report. The teacher needs to know right away that you plan to be a partner in this process.

As you prepare your report, be careful to explain any terminology you have learned in this book that might be unfamiliar to the teacher.

Another sheet in the packet is a review of the parent-teacher conference. The meeting will be most productive if you take the time to write down your goals before you go; then evaluate what was achieved after you get home.

Parent-Teacher Teamwork

Stephen was in the middle of the third grading period

when he decided the most important thing in the world was baseball. As baseball increasingly consumed his time, his grades began to slide. To keep his parents from finding out he was slacking off, he complained to them, "This work is too hard. My teacher never gives me enough time to finish it." In his mind, this was not a fib. He had rationalized to the point where he didn't feel responsible for his failings any more. It seemed natural to project his problem onto the teacher.

An uninformed parent might have accepted Stephen's complaints and sided with him, murmuring, "He shouldn't treat you like that. If you can't get the work done, that's O.K." Stephen's parents, however, knew how their son operated and they had a good relationship with his teacher.

Since Stephen was a Promoter who functioned at about Level 2 and needed close supervision, they called the teacher and asked him about Stephen's comments. Mr. O'Neill laughed and told them, "Your son's problem isn't overwork, it's over-zealousness for baseball. He spends a lot of class time rapping with the other boys about it. I've had several talks with him." That conversation led to concrete plans to hold Stephen accountable for his lying and help him set better priorities for his time. Within a week and a half his performance was back where it belonged.

When your children know that you have regular contact with their teachers and serve as their consultant, they will have little opportunity to manipulate situations for their own good. Children with Promoter personality styles are the ones most likely to do that, but others have been known to try it as well.

Parents need to keep lines of communication with the teacher open both ways. If Mr. O'Neill had alerted the parents earlier, Stephen would not have found himself in so much trouble. Parents know when things aren't going well, but they don't always know the cause. Frequent, positive interaction between parents and teachers is in the best interests of the child.

You are now ready to use your appendix/packet to prepare a profile of your child for a teacher's meeting or home schooling. May God encourage you about your children as you come to know them better.

Chapter Twelve

Choosing A Career

"What do you want to be when you grow up?"

Chances are, you and your child's aunts, uncles, cousins, grandparents, and teachers have been asking him that question ever since he learned to talk. In the early years, it is one of the games of childhood: play that you're a doctor, a teacher, a Hollywood star, a missionary. About the time of adolescence, however, it isn't such a game any more. Parents begin checking their bank accounts and their children's course schedules and quiz their blossoming teenagers in earnest: "What do you want to do with your life?"

We have put this chapter at the end of the book so you can see how the lifetime you have spent in raising your children can come to fruition in this time of decision.

Without God, young people make career choices that can have tragic consequences, as we shall see later. With God, they may make a few false starts along the way, but if they will listen, there is always Someone behind them saying, "This is the way, walk in it" (Isa. 30:21 NASB).

If you are like most parents, you have a few basic questions troubling you concerning your child's future. Perhaps you feel that you have failed in a few areas yourself, and you don't want them to fall into the same pits. You may see young people in America straying off into drugs, crime, and immorality, making no effort to earn a living, and wonder how your child will be different.

With God's guidance, you and your child can make a great deal of difference in their future. Many tools are available to help you shape it. If you have given your child a foundation on the rock of Christ, his house will stand firm when the rains descend and the floods come in.

God says to your child, "I have called you by name; you are Mine" (Isa. 43:1 NASB). He promises, "I will lead the blind by a way they do not know, in paths they do not know I will guide them. I will make darkness into light before them and rugged places into plains. These are the things I will do, and I will not leave them undone" (Isa. 42:16 NASB).

All parents ask similar questions as the decision time approaches:

Will my child be successful?
Will he make costly mistakes?
Will he make money? Will money become his god?
Will he stop going to church?
Will he be happy?
Should I steer my child into full-time Christian ministry?
Shall I insist that my child go to college?
Will he make decisions as I would have made them?
Will he choose the college and career that I think are best for him?

Consider the story of Jeff. His father, brothers, and uncles were all active policemen and expected him to become one, too. When he expressed doubts, his father said, "Jeff, what else are you going to do? You can't let down the community. They expect us to uphold our tradition. I know that bunch of liberals who teach at your college have no use for us, but don't you listen to them. If they were real men, they wouldn't be working as teachers."

Jeff, who had a Server personality, couldn't see himself as a policeman, but his father said he would like it if he understood all its different dimensions. The pressure was overwhelming. His mother didn't interfere, because over the years she had learned it was better to "go along to get along." Jeff had learned to adopt the same style when it came to his father.

Although he had a secret dream of becoming a counselor in a church, to please his father he agreed to enter the police academy. He rationalized that he should have lots of opportunities to counsel hurting people in the course of his work.

When Jeff graduated from the police academy, he was assigned to a squad car. His partner, a fifteen-year veteran, quickly poured cold water on Jeff's counseling ideas. "If you make yourself vulnerable, you're just asking to be hurt," he said. "Don't waste your time trying to solve family disputes or counsel first offenders. The way to deal with lawbreakers is to be tough."

Jeff cringed at his attitude and whenever he had the opportunity, tried to talk to someone. Invariably, his partner told him to quit wasting time. "We need to get back on the street," he said gruffly. "They aren't paying us to play nursemaid."

At the end of Jeff's first year he knew that he was a failure as a police officer and was completely frustrated in his desire to help people. He began to lose weight and became despondent. One day his father said, "Jeff, the other officers on the force are real concerned about you. They say you don't keep your mind on what you're doing, and they're afraid if you don't change, you'll get someone killed."

Jeff looked at his father for a long while and finally said, "They're right. My heart is just not in it. I feel like a total failure."

His dad said quietly, "I pushed you real hard to become a policeman. I thought that once you tried it, you'd love it like everyone else has. I guess I was wrong. If this work is not for you, then you have my blessing to resign. I'm sorry I pushed you, but police work was the only way I knew. I just wanted you to have a job that would provide for your family."

That was the first time Jeff realized that his dad was only interested in his well being. It was one of the few times his father recognized the bad results of his own domineering style. Their relationship improved greatly after this honest exchange, and Jeff changed careers

Jeff's father made the same mistake as many parents. He placed top priority on a career that would provide security. In a way, he was placing his son back at Level 1 instead of realizing that he had to outgrow that kind of immature motivation. He was not seeking God's will for his son's life but playing God on his behalf. This can have long-lasting implications, both in the present and eternally.

Every young person needs to set his own timeclock for attending to the stewardship of his talents. Parents should not make college or technical school an issue. Higher education is a ticket to a destination, not an end in itself. Sometimes a young person can learn more about life from a few years' experience in a trade than he could in the hothouse environment of a college campus. Your child is about to enroll in the School of Lifelong Learning. By choosing what courses to take in this School, he will add vibrancy to his life as he is forced to seek God's will continually.

Parents cannot live their children's lives for them. They must not force them into jobs or careers simply because they are appropriate in their own eyes. A career decision should be made by the person involved, with good information and guidance from parents but no insistent pressure.

Jeff is an example of those whose stories are repeated countless times throughout our nation: individuals locked in jobs and careers that are not compatible with their gifts and talents, people living from weekend to weekend as they endure their work. Often the price paid for such unhappiness is destructive not only to the individual and his self-esteem but also to other family members.

The question then becomes: Can parents do anything to ensure that their children choose careers that will be appropriate for them? The answer is that although parents cannot guarantee their children's career happiness, they can provide the guidance that will give them every opportunity to make the right choice. For too long this guidance has been left solely to professionals in the schools who have minimal contact with our children. They have access to information on colleges and careers, but it is impossible for them to have the insight that parents have gained over a period of several years.

The greatest thing parents can do in the younger years to prepare their children for careers is to help them develop the proper attitudes toward God and toward work. They need to learn that God is their Provider, Counselor, and Friend. He is the source of their self-esteem, not their career. God intends for their work to be a blessing, not a curse. He will guide them into work that puts to good use the gifts He has placed within them. He does not guarantee great wealth, but He does guarantee to provide their daily bread. Jesus said, "Seek ye first the kingdom of God, and his righteousness; and all these things shall be added unto you" (Matt. 6:33 KJV).

In today's society, too many children have low levels of aspiration because during their growing years they knew only frustration and heartache with little parental support and encouragement. When this happens, a child will take any career that is offered, not because that is what he desires, but because he thinks he may not get any other offers. Unhappy in his work, he will switch from job to job, never satisfied and never feeling valued.

All of the chapters in this book can be used to help you prepare your child for a career. Preparation does not begin in college or even in high school. It begins when a small child learns to respect other people and their differences, when he learns how to speak and how to listen, when his character is developed and his self-esteem increased, when he contributes to the work of the household and learns to be a disciple.

As you help your children to grow in the grace and knowledge of Jesus Christ and take on His traits, you are preparing them to fulfill God's call on their lives. Their career choices will become easier and they will be willing to commit themselves to getting an education or developing the technical skills they need.

Career Options for Your Child

To get some idea of the careers your children might prefer, review their personality traits.

Because a Ruler . . .
   Likes challenges
   Is an original thinker
   Is results-oriented
   Likes to be in charge
   Dislikes menial, repetitious jobs
   Doesn't like constraints on his plans and
      activities
   Is more concerned with tasks than people . . .
Rulers tend to choose these occupations:
   Managers
   Entrepreneurs
   Military officers
   Business executives

Because a Designer . . .

    Is conscientious

    Likes to be precise

    Controls the environment by organizing things

    Places a high standard on work expectations

    Likes to analyze and solve problems

    Tends to emphasize tasks more than people . . .

Designers tend to choose these occupations:

    Accountant

    Business manager

    Researcher

    Planner

Because a Promoter . . .

    Likes social interaction

    Tends to be optimistic

    Is persuasive

    Dislikes detail and paperwork

    Desires to be popular

    Enjoys challenges, especially involving people

    Is more concerned with people than tasks . . .

Promoters tend to choose these occupations:

    Marketing

    Consulting

    Sales

Because a Server . . .

    Enjoys productive routines

    Likes to be part of a group

    Tends to be deliberate in approaching tasks

    Has a gentle manner

    Is stressed by change and unstable environments

    Needs a friendly environment

    Is more concerned with people than with task . . .

Servers tend to choose these careers:

    Counselor

    Teacher

    Personnel Officer

Here is a more detailed chart rating potential for job satisfaction by personality style.

JOB SATISFACTION BASED ON PERSONALITY				
OCCUPATION	RULER	DESIGNER	PROMOTER	SERVER
Manager	E	E-F	E-G	F-P
Accountant, Personnel Officer	F	E	G	G-E
Engineer, Architect	G	E	P	F
Computer Operator, Scientist, Mathematician	F	E	P	G
Social Scientist, Religious or Social Worker	F-P	F	G	E
Lawyer	E-G	E	G-F	F
Teacher	F	E	E-G	G-E
Physician	E-G	E	F-P	G
Health Technician	G-F	E	G-P	E-G
Writer, Artist	F-P	E	E-G	F-P
Entertainer	G	G-F	E	F-P
Marketer, Salesman	G-F	G-F	E	G
Clerk	F-G	E	F-P	G
Policeman, Fireman	E	G	G-F	F-P
Auto Mechanic	G	E	F-P	G-F
Tradesman	G	E	F-P	G-F
(Code: E = Excellent match; G = Good match; F = Fair match; P = Poor match.)				

Trying Out a Career

As your children grow up, they will express interest in many types of jobs. These interests will come and go, depending on what the other children are talking about, or what TV program is popular. It is a good idea to show interest in any career that interests your children and to help them find out more information on it. Never discourage them from investigating a career, even if deep down you know that type of role would be difficult for them to handle, given their personality.

When your child enters his adolescent years, the choices he makes about careers will tend to be more directed than they were when he was younger, although they still may reflect a lot of peer influence. When you sense that your child is becoming serious about a particular career, help him to meet people who are involved in that field and spend time observing what they do. Find out what kind of education is required and where it can be obtained. Encourage him to get a volunteer or part-time job doing similar work to see if he likes it.

Here are suggestions for pre-career activities that can give your child a taste of the real thing. They are divided into four categories as defined by D. J. Prediger: data, ideas, people, and things.

PRE-CAREER ACTIVITIES

DATA
(impersonal processes using
facts, records, files, numbers)

PRE-CAREER ACTIVITIES
    Secretary or treasurer for youth group
    Paper route
    Buyer for church or school organization

Home computer
Cashier
Typing papers for school
Assembly line work
Job and college applications for friends
Research on a variety of careers
Library aide

CAREER CHOICES
Purchasing agent
Secretary
Accountant
Air traffic controller
Computer programmer
Librarian

IDEAS
(words, music, abstractions, theories)

PRE-CAREER ACTIVITIES
Church or school newspapers and magazines
Band, orchestra, or chorus
Church choir or ensemble
Debating club
Lobbying Congress or serving as aide
Experimenting with chemistry set
Art lessons
Decorating the family home
Photography
Short story and poetry contest
Dance

CAREER CHOICES
Scientist
Musician
Philosopher

College professor
Artist
Interior designer
Graphic designer

People
(helping, serving, persuading, entertaining, motivating, changing behavior)

Pre-career Activities
Sales clerk
Sunday school teacher
Tutor for younger children or illiterate adults
Hospital or nursing home volunteer or aide
Day care or babysitting
Food or clothing distributor to the poor
Summer recreation aide
Counselor at camp or vacation Bible school
Subscription sales person
Teacher's aide
Fast food worker
Supermarket bagger
Assistant to church pastors and staff

Career Choices
Pastor
Teacher
Salesperson
Nurse or doctor
Occupational therapist

Things
(machinery, repairs, physical processes)

PRE-CAREER ACTIVITIES
   Gardening
   Drafting
   Construction
   Motel or house cleaning
   Mowing lawns
   Weather or astronomy observation
   Clerk in photo shop
   Model cars and planes
   Making own clothes
   Gas station
   Buying old car and fixing it up
   Fixing broken appliances around the house

CAREER CHOICES
   Car mechanic
   Farmer
   Draftsman or engineer
   Bricklayer
   Meteorologist or astronomer
   Repairman for cameras, appliances, televisions
   Seamstress, tailor, clothing designer
   Newspaper press operator

Subtleties of Parental Guidance

How will you know which of these categories interests your child? You will do what you have always done: listen to your children and watch how they spend their time. Here is one family's experience.

As the parents of several children, Carle and Martha had lived through many of their children's vocational interest changes. Under the influence of her friends, their daughter Cassie seemed to be drifting toward a career choice that they both felt was wrong for her. She had little interest in college, and they were not inclined to pay for technical school unless there was a strong interest there.

Carle began listening more closely to Cassie so he could assess what interested her personally, rather than what interested her friends. That evening at the dinner table Carle said, "Cassie, I saw you out in the yard today with the three Jordan children. What were they doing over here so far from home?"

"They come over every time they see me out in the yard," Cassie said enthusiastically. "They like to tell me about their new puppies and what they're doing in school."

Carle thought, "She seems to fit in the 'people' category." Aloud he said, "How did you get so friendly with those kids?"

"One morning when I was jogging in the park, they were there and I started talking with them and pushing them on the swings. Then I taught them how to climb the ropes."

"I didn't know you could climb ropes," Carle said with surprise.

"Oh, yeah. I do it all the time," Cassie said. "I like to get out in the open and work hard." Carle realized that Cassie's physical activity and recreational skills showed her interest in the "things" category as well. She showed no interest in "data" or "ideas."

Before he tried to give Cassie any suggestions about a career, Carle decided to educate himself. He went to the library and looked in the Dictionary of Occupational Titles, a publication of the Department of Labor, for job opportunities that seemed to fit Cassie's interests in children and outdoor activities. One career that struck him was that of a recreation supervisor, people who are in demand for city projects, camps, private organizations, and schools for handicapped youngsters.

Because he knew his daughter well, Carle didn't try to present his findings to her all at once. He knew he might be wrong and also wanted to give her the freedom to discover her calling for herself without pressure from him. At home that night, he mentioned casually to Cassie that he had seen a newspaper ad for summer work with the local recreation department.

"What do they do? Just babysit the kids?" Cassie asked.

"Actually, they don't," said Carle. "They do a lot of teaching and help the children develop their athletic skills, just like you did when you taught the Jordan kids how to climb the rope."

"Really?" said Cassie. "That might be kind of fun. How do you apply?" Carle gave her the information, and the next day Cassie went to fill out an application. When she came home, she was absolutely delighted. The director had apparently taken a liking to her and offered her a job immediately. The experience opened up a whole new world to Cassie and sent her on the way to a career that she loved.

Most families rely on school counselors who have special training to guide their children in their career searches. You can take advantage of such services, but don't neglect your own participation as a parent. No guidance or vocational counselors will ever have the interest you have in your child or the knowledge that you have gained in a lifetime of raising him. Very few will be interested in seeking God's will on their behalf.

If these counselors make recommendations, be sure that you know what they are suggesting and what is the basis for their decision. Like Jeff's father in the earlier story, the counselor may be suggesting a career mainly because it will have many job openings in the next few years. It may fit your child's talents but not be the career that you and your child feel the Lord is calling him to.

When God has a calling on your child's life, He will make a way where there is no way. Seek His will with your child, looking for at least "two or three witnesses" to confirm it. God leads through circumstances, through prayer and revelation, through the advice of others, and through His Word. Even children can be trained to hear His voice if they have taken the step of submitting their will to His. Although any child can grow up to become wealthy, the proof that God has guided him will not be material prosperity but whether his work brings glory to God.

The Difference that Faith Makes

As Perry left the Divorce Court, his life in ruins, he said to himself, "Where did I go wrong? I worked hard, I tried to be a good husband, but everything I did turned to dust."

Recently we had the opportunity to talk with Perry about the traumatic events that brought him to that point in his life. He was willing to talk to us because of the changes that have occurred since that day.

"Ever since I can remember," Perry said, "I always tried to please my father, but he had such high standards I could never meet them. He always noticed the Bs on my report card instead of the As. After a baseball game he would say, 'Perry, I saw a lot of improvement out there today, but you could even do better if you would . . .'"

"Dad would criticize the activities I liked by saying such things as, 'You spend too much time socializing when you could be practicing the piano.' He never seemed to understand that I enjoyed being around people. I would do anything, even chores or unpleasant jobs, if I had someone to talk to."

In Perry's effort to please his unpleasable father, he gave up his preferred subjects in school in order to take the technical subjects his father preferred. Since his father ridiculed people in sales and public relations as "glad handers" who had no skills, he abandoned those fields as career options.

When his father died, Perry took over the family's custom home design business. "Over the course of about ten years I got married and started a family," he said. "The firm prospered, and I was initially caught up in the business and its rapid growth. After about three years, though, hard times hit, and suddenly I realized how much I hated what I was doing. Unfortunately, I didn't face up to my feelings. I tried to escape through alcohol. You know the rest."

Perry's business failed, his marriage fell apart, and he entered an alcoholic treatment center. That was when his life began to turn around. During that time he accepted Jesus Christ as his Lord and Savior, and ever since then he has rebuilt his life. Miraculously, even his marriage was restored. He is now in a totally different line of work.

"When I began getting my life back together," he said, "I spent a lot of time praying and seeking God about what kind of work I should be doing. I just couldn't face going back to my former profession. Now that I knew there was a God who loved me, I was absolutely convinced that He would place me in an occupation that I would love."

"The career counseling I received showed me I needed a job that would allow me to meet people and work with them. That's how I ended up in a sales and marketing firm. I can't tell you how happy I am. My whole life seems brighter, and I know I'm more pleasant to be around; I enjoy my family, and I look forward to going to work."

All of us have seen these scenarios played out in the lives of our friends and neighbors. Maybe you are having a similar experience in your own life. The work that we do is such a vital part of us that unless our career fits in with God's plan we will be miserable.

Choosing a career is not a game of chance. Many tools are available to find options for any individual. The greatest resource, however, is the knowledge that God rules in the lives of men, women, and children. He who delights himself in the Lord is "like a tree planted by streams of water, which yields its fruit in season and whose leaf does not wither. Whatever he does prospers" (Ps. 1:3 NIV).

Conclusion

Jesus gave us a wonderful command, "Love one another." He gave us the power through His Spirit to obey this command. It has been our intent to share with you some practical ways to love one another, including our differences, in our twentieth century culture.

Of course, learning to "love one another" by knowing and appreciating differences in gifts, personalities, and development is a process. It doesn't happen overnight. It is our hope that with continual prayer, this book will help you and your family as you travel the road to loving one another consistently, constantly, and practically.

APPENDIX/PACKET

CURRENT RELIABILITY AND VALIDITY OF THE RESEARCH

Preliminary research has been conducted on the following instruments used in *Loving Our Differences.*

- Levels of Motivation Test (chapter one)
- Functional Gifts Test (chapter two)
- Personality Test (chapter three)

The instrument measuring Motivational Levels (packet, chapter one) has a high degree of validity, with some caution advised in interpreting the distinction between Levels 2 and 3. Because these levels tend to vary according to environmental factors, we feel that exercising caution in defining these levels enhances the value and validity of the instrument. To find the most likely position of a Level 2 or 3 individual, look for consistent trends over a period of two to three weeks.

The Functional Gifts Test (packet, chapter two) was developed from instruments used in various churches around the nation and from the Houts Motivational Gift Test, which has been extensively researched. Its reliability correlates highly with the Houts Test and with the constructs linking personality and motivational gifts described in chapter two.

The Personality Inventory in the packet (chapter three) was based partially on research conducted by such renowned individuals as Merrill and Reid (1980), Bernice McCarthy (1980), Raymond Cattell (1965), and H. Eysenck (1947). Some of the researchers developed their own instruments, with reliability ratings exceeding .80. The Personality instrument in *Loving Our Differences*, on a limited population, showed a reliability rating of .85. Although it is too early to make a definitive statement, this would indicate that the instrument has a very high level of reliability. It must be kept in mind that the Personality Inventory was designed to indicate the one or two personality tendencies that an individual is most likely to display under most circumstances.

FAMILY QUIZZES, ACTIVITIES

The following pages include a sample of family activities to help you discover your gifts and differences. These quizzes are also provided in a separate packet in multiple copies for use with your family. The packet may be purchased from your local bookstore or by writing CBN Publishing.

PACKET: CHAPTER ONE
Motivational Development Inventory

Directions:

Think of the individual being rated as he would act in one particular setting such as home, school, or work. As you carefully consider each question, ask yourself, "Is he/she most like this, least like this, or somewhere in between?" Circle the appropriate number. Number 5 means "most of the time," number 3 means "sometimes," and number 1 means "rarely or never." Keep in mind that you are describing current behavior, not the way the individual acted in the past.

Part 1: Rating a Child

Statement	Score
	Mostly Rarely
1. He/she wants his own way.	5 4 3 2 1
2. He/she will say, "Hey, look at me!"	5 4 3 2 1
3. He/she wants respect for his ideas.	5 4 3 2 1
4. He/she searches for opportunities to help others.	5 4 3 2 1
5. He/she will do most tasks if verbally praised for his efforts.	5 4 3 2 1
6. He/she often praises peers even in their absence.	5 4 3 2 1
7. He/she is loyal and will stand up for family or friends.	5 4 3 2 1
8. He/she is known by friends as somewhat of a "show-off."	5 4 3 2 1
9. He/she has a very short attention span and changes activities often.	5 4 3 2 1
10. He/she is self-motivated to complete work for the satisfaction gained from being productive.	5 4 3 2 1
11. He/she frequently says, "No, that's mine!"	5 4 3 2 1
12. He/she will play with others' toys and possessions without asking.	5 4 3 2 1
13. He/she willingly volunteers for needed tasks.	5 4 3 2 1
14. He/she will become angry and throw a temper tantrum if he does not get what he wants immediately.	5 4 3 2 1
15. He/she is even-tempered and self-controlled.	5 4 3 2 1
16. He/she enjoys organized group activities.	5 4 3 2 1
17. He/she is able to make some objective decisions.	5 4 3 2 1
18. He/she demands that his achievements be placed on display for others to admire.	5 4 3 2 1
19. He/she enjoys participating in competitive activities, but is upset if his efforts are not recognized.	5 4 3 2 1

20. He/she has a healthy appreciation of rules and likes firmness in adults.   5 4 3 2 1
21. He/she strives for competence in his tasks.   5 4 3 2 1
22. He/she is quick to judge peers' behavior.   5 4 3 2 1
23. He/she will behave most appropriately when attention is centered on him.   5 4 3 2 1
24. He/she enjoys being a part of a particular group.   5 4 3 2 1
25. He/she can carry on a good conversation with adults on an adult level.   5 4 3 2 1
26. He/she enjoys the company of adults, both family and others.   5 4 3 2 1
27. He/she will lose interest in an activity if someone is not there watching and encouraging him.   5 4 3 2 1
28. He/she is continually optimistic despite trying circumstances.   5 4 3 2 1
29. He/she is able to stand up for what he believes is right even in the face of criticism.   5 4 3 2 1
30. He/she will become interested in certain subjects, activities, or hobbies in order to win approval.   5 4 3 2 1
31. He/she becomes unusually upset when others disagree with him.   5 4 3 2 1
32. He/she must be told specifically what is expected before he is able to comply.   5 4 3 2 1

Part 2: Rating an Adolescent or Adult

Statement	Score	
	Mostly	Rarely
1. He/she wants his own way.	5 4 3 2 1	
2. He/she will say, "Hey, look at me!"	5 4 3 2 1	
3. He/she wants respect for his ideas as well as approval.	5 4 3 2 1	
4. He/she searches for opportunities to help others.	5 4 3 2 1	
5. He/she will do most tasks if verbally praised for his efforts.	5 4 3 2 1	
6. He/she often praises peers even in their absence.	5 4 3 2 1	
7. He/she is loyal and will stand up for family, friends, company, or ministry.	5 4 3 2 1	
8. He/she is known by friends or workmates as somewhat of a "show off."	5 4 3 2 1	
9. He/she has a very short attention span and changes activities often.	5 4 3 2 1	
10. He/she is self-motivated to complete		

work for the satisfaction gained from being productive.	5	4	3	2	1
11. He/she frequently says,"I know my rights. I don't have to do it if I don't want to."	5	4	3	2	1
12. He/she will use others' tools and equipment without asking.	5	4	3	2	1
13. He/she willingly volunteers for needed tasks.	5	4	3	2	1
14. He/she will become angry and throw a temper tantrum if he does not get what he wants immediately.	5	4	3	2	1
15. He/she is even-tempered and self-controlled.	5	4	3	2	1
16. He/she enjoys organized group activities.	5	4	3	2	1
17. He/she is very generous with his time and possessions.	5	4	3	2	1
18. He/she demands that his achievements be placed on display for others to admire.	5	4	3	2	1
19. He/she enjoys participating in competitive activities, but is upset if his efforts are not recognized.	5	4	3	2	1
20. He/she has a healthy appreciation of rules and likes firmness in adults.	5	4	3	2	1
21. He/she strives for competence in his tasks.	5	4	3	2	1
22. He/she is quick to judge peers' behavior.	5	4	3	2	1
23. He/she will behave most appropriately when attention is centered on him.	5	4	3	2	1
24. He/she enjoys being a part of a particular group.	5	4	3	2	1
25. He/she can carry on a good conversation with adults on an adult level.	5	4	3	2	1
26. He/she enjoys the company of family and others.	5	4	3	2	1
27. He/she will lose interest in an activity if someone is not there watching and encouraging him.	5	4	3	2	1
28. He/she is continually optimistic despite trying circumstances.	5	4	3	2	1
29. He/she is able to stand up for what he believes is right, even in the face of criticism.	5	4	3	2	1
30. He/she will become interested in certain projects or activities if immediate and tangible benefits result.	5	4	3	2	1
31. He/she becomes unusually upset when others disagree with him.	5	4	3	2	1
32. He/she must be told specifically what is expected before he is able to comply.	5	4	3	2	1

Score Sheet for Levels of Motivation

Directions:
Take the score (from 1 to 5) for each question above and enter it on the appropriate line below. When you have filled in every space, add the numbers across each line and write in the totals.

LEVEL 1
Item	1	9	11	12	14	30	31	32	Totals
Score	__	__	__	__	__	__	__	__	____

LEVEL 2
Item	2	5	8	18	19	22	23	27	
Score	__	__	__	__	__	__	__	__	____

LEVEL 3
Item	3	7	15	16	20	21	24	26	
Score	__	__	__	__	__	__	__	__	____

LEVEL 4
Item	4	6	10	13	17	25	28	29	
Score	__	__	__	__	__	__	__	__	____

Rank the Levels according to their totals, from the highest to the lowest.
Highest total: Level ___   Second highest total: Level ___
Third highest total: Level ___   Lowest total: Level ___

The highest and second highest scores suggest the person's usual level of motivation in a particular setting.

PACKET: CHAPTER TWO

This questionnaire is designed to assist you in discovering the gifts God has given you, as described in Romans 12:6-8.

As you complete this questionnaire, try to check the box that best describes your behavior in most situations. Do not overly analyze your answer, but respond as to the way you generally feel.

Directions:
1. Read through the list of 70 statements and place a check beside those responses which best describe you.
2. After completing the questionnaire, transfer the numerical value of your answers to the Tabulation Chart at the end of the test; then add the scores horizontally in each line and record the total at the right.
3. The total will give you an idea of your spiritual gifts. Your primary functional gift should be indicated by your largest number of points. Your secondary functional gift should have the second highest total, and so on, through the seven gifts.
4. This test will give you an idea of the intensity of your gifts and will also give you an idea of where you might need to grow. Remember that all of the gifts are available to us as we earnestly seek to do His will and submit ourselves to Him.

	Usually True (5)	Sometimes True (3)	Seldom True (1)	Rarely True (0)
1. You enjoy assisting people with their personal and emotional problems.				
2. You enjoy motivating others to various tasks and ministries.				
3. You concentrate more on practical things that need to done rather than the reasons.				
4. You immediately offer your services when people are in need.				
5. You would rather give money than do practical kinds of things.				
6. You like to visit people who are sick or disabled.				
7. You feel that your belief and conviction in spiritual things exceeds most other people's.				
8. You usually know whether something is right or wrong.				
9. You speak out to correct things that are not quite correct.				
10. People look to you for practical advice on personal issues.				
11. You respond quickly to problems by taking positive, practical steps to bring a successful conclusion.				
12. People often come to you with difficult problems and questions which require biblical understanding.				
13. You feel a real responsibility to provide direction to people and organizations.				
14. You take a lot of satisfaction in just doing for others.				
15. You like to lay things out in a way that helps people become more effective.				
16. Your first response to someone in need is to send money.				
17. When you know someone is hurting, you feel an immediate burden to bring them some encouragement and cheer.				
18. When times are tough, you are resolute in trusting God.				
19. You are able to determine other people's motives and intentions, even when you have recently met them.				
20. You have a tendency to speak-upwhen controversial issues are being dealt with in a group.				

	Usually True (5)	Sometimes True (3)	Seldom True (1)	Rarely True (0)
21. You enjoy searching for answers, particularly in the Bible.				
22. You see yourself in a supportive role to others but not generally in a place of leadership.				
23. You look for opportunities to give money, regardless of whether a request has been made.				
24. You are able to express joy even in the presence of those who are suffering.				
25. You enjoy investigating the deeper truths of the Bible.				
26. You generally see the overall scope of a project and can determine what needs to be done.				
27. You are able to communicate easily with people who are experiencing much suffering.				
28. You get a great deal of joy in giving, regardless of the response you receive.				
29. You feel real love and compassion for people having personal and emotional problems.				
30. When you give your advice to someone, you emphasize the "how" rather than the "why."				
31. You seem to have an ability to know and understand the things of God's Word.				
32. You have a special concern in helping people reach their aspirations.				
33. People seem to depend upon you to make the major decisions for others.				
34. You are satisfied more with how a person has been helped rather than what you personally may have done.				
35. You prefer to give money anonymously.				
36. You prefer to minister to those who are suffering physically or emotionally.				
37. You see the opportunity to have people in your home as exciting rather than as a responsibility.				
38. You like to explain the meaning of things rather than give a global response.				
39. You prefer to listen to people's problems rather than share your own.				
40. People see you as a person with answers to situations that are personally difficult.				
41. You usually take the leadership in a group where none exists.				
42. To you, money given does not require an appreciative response as long as you feel led to give.				

	Usually True (5)	Sometimes True (3)	Seldom True (1)	Rarely True (0)
43. You can sense love and are very vulnerable to hurt from lack of love.				
44. You feel a great deal of compassion for those who are in physical or emotional need and desire to help them in some way.				
45. You have a tendency to encourage people when you see they are discouraged.				
46. You cannot stand to allow things that are wrong and sinful to go unexposed.				
47. You tend to organize your thoughts very systematically.				
48. Your decisions and advice to people have generally proven to be worthwhile and valuable.				
49. You enjoy sharing difficult verses and passages of Scripture with people in an understandable way.				
50. You often find yourself being responsible for making decisions on behalf of groups or organizations.				
51. You enjoy doing for others without being asked.				
52. You are always alert to assist people.				
53. You see the giving of money as a special ministry God has given you.				
54. You take great joy in helping people who are in physical distress.				
55. You have witnessed God do mighty things in your life which others believed could not be done but you always did.				
56. When you speak to believers, you tend to share Scripture and insightful teaching rather than personal experiences.				
57. You tend to enjoy ministering to individuals rather than groups.				
58. You enjoy and sense a responsibility to clarify confusion and misunderstanding of Scripture.				
59. You seem to know what practical needs people have often without asking.				
60. You like being placed in the position of having to make the final decision for groups or organizations.				
61. You often do nitty gritty jobs as a means of freeing people to do things that they desire to do.				
62. You enjoy being involved in financial projects.				

230

	Usually True (5)	Sometimes True (3)	Seldom True (1)	Rarely True(0)
63. You are more than willing to spend time or money to help people who are suffering.				
64. You tend to be a good judge of people's behavior even when others have an opposite view.				
65. You would rather do a job yourself than have to work with a group.				
66. Regardless of your personal feelings, you feel obligated to help someone when he has a need.				
67. When you give, you do so generously without thought of the cost involved.				
68. You often seem to have a deeper understanding of God's Word than people who have been in the Word longer.				
69. When discussing a point with others, you appeal to their logic and reason rather than simply to their emotion.				
70. People tend to depend on your discernment in issues of right and wrong.				

TABULATION CHART

										TOTALS	
1	6	17	54	24	27	29	36	44	43		Mercy
2	13	15	26	33	34	41	47	50	60		Leadership
3	4	14	22	51	52	59	61	65	66		Service
5	16	23	28	35	42	53	62	63	67		Giving
7	8	9	18	19	20	46	55	64	70		Prophecy
10	11	30	32	37	39	40	45	48	57		Exhortation
12	21	25	31	38	49	56	58	68	69		Teaching

PACKET: CHAPTER THREE
Personality Tendency Inventory

Name_____

Date_____

Introduction:

This Personality Tendency Inventory is designed to give you a general idea of your personality and communication style. It is not an in-depth personality assessment, but it will give you some insight about yourself and the way you relate to others. The instrument can also be used to evaluate others, although you must be careful not to use it unwisely or unkindly.

You will need this information to make the best use of succeeding chapters in *Loving Our Differences*. In future chapters we will use this information to help you understand how you come across to others, how you or your child learns best, how to delegate household chores, how to discipline effectively and lovingly, and how to choose careers.

Directions:

Think of yourself or the person you are evaluating in one particular setting (home, work, school, etc.).

Read the descriptive word. Decide if you would always describe yourself or the person in that way, would never use that description, or sometimes yes and sometimes no. Make a choice from numbers 1 to 7, from "That's not me!" to "That's me!" Don't be afraid of sounding boastful. Just try to see yourself as God sees you, with your gifts as well as the areas where God isn't finished with you yet. We all have Christ-like qualities that are to be used for God's purposes and we also have areas needing growth.

Circle the number that describes you best. Remember to think of yourself or the person you are evaluating in only one particular setting.

	That's Me	That's Not Me		That's Me	That's Not Me
1. Sincere	7 6 5 4 3 2 1		19. Open-minded	7 6 5 4 3 2 1	
2. Routine	7 6 5 4 3 2 1		20. Compassionate	7 6 5 4 3 2 1	
3. Assertive	7 6 5 4 3 2 1		21. Prevailing	7 6 5 4 3 2 1	
4. Systematic	7 6 5 4 3 2 1		22. Shy	7 6 5 4 3 2 1	
5. Planner	7 6 5 4 3 2 1		23. Constant	7 6 5 4 3 2 1	
6. Expressive	7 6 5 4 3 2 1		24. Direct	7 6 5 4 3 2 1	
7. Optimistic	7 6 5 4 3 2 1		25. Careful	7 6 5 4 3 2 1	
8. Humble	7 6 5 4 3 2 1		26. Tender-hearted	7 6 5 4 3 2 1	
9. Animated	7 6 5 4 3 2 1		27. Reserved	7 6 5 4 3 2 1	
10. Restless	7 6 5 4 3 2 1		28. Firm	7 6 5 4 3 2 1	
11. Detailed	7 6 5 4 3 2 1		29. Outgoing	7 6 5 4 3 2 1	
12. Cheerful	7 6 5 4 3 2 1		30. Practical	7 6 5 4 3 2 1	
13. Accommodating	7 6 5 4 3 2 1		31. Empathetic	7 6 5 4 3 2 1	
14. Aggressive	7 6 5 4 3 2 1		32. Caretaker	7 6 5 4 3 2 1	
15. Restrained	7 6 5 4 3 2 1		33. Leader	7 6 5 4 3 2 1	
16. Exacting	7 6 5 4 3 2 1		34. Adventurous	7 6 5 4 3 2 1	
17. Decisive	7 6 5 4 3 2 1		35. Critiquing	7 6 5 4 3 2 1	
18. Persuasive	7 6 5 4 3 2 1		36. Productive	7 6 5 4 3 2 1	

37.Flexible	7 6 5 4 3 2 1
38.Opinionated	7 6 5 4 3 2 1
39.Independent	7 6 5 4 3 2 1
40.Sheltering	7 6 5 4 3 2 1
41.Enjoyable	7 6 5 4 3 2 1
42.Perfectionist	7 6 5 4 3 2 1
43.Changeable	7 6 5 4 3 2 1
44.Ordered	7 6 5 4 3 2 1
45.Analytical	7 6 5 4 3 2 1
46.Stable	7 6 5 4 3 2 1
47.Talkative	7 6 5 4 3 2 1
48.Demonstrative	7 6 5 4 3 2 1

49.Competitive	7 6 5 4 3 2 1
50.Original	7 6 5 4 3 2 1
51.Gentle	7 6 5 4 3 2 1
52.Tactful	7 6 5 4 3 2 1
53.Confident	7 6 5 4 3 2 1
54.Competent	7 6 5 4 3 2 1
55.Questioning	7 6 5 4 3 2 1
56.Result-oriented	7 6 5 4 3 2 1
57.Impulsive	7 6 5 4 3 2 1
58.Relaxed	7 6 5 4 3 2 1
59.Thorough	7 6 5 4 3 2 1
60.Steadying	7 6 5 4 3 2 1

Personality Tendency Scoring Sheet

Directions:

Copy your responses from the personality survey onto the appropriate line below. For example, if you scored yourself as "4" on question 3, write in a "4" on the first line under Ruler.

After you have transferred all the scores from the questions to the grid, add each line and enter the total in the space provided.

RULER

‾3 ‾10 ‾14 ‾17 ‾21 ‾24 ‾28 ‾33 ‾34 ‾36 ‾38 ‾39 ‾49 ‾53 ‾56 Total

Divide Total by 15 to get average score in Ruler category: _____

DESIGNER

‾4 ‾5 ‾11 ‾13 ‾15 ‾16 ‾23 ‾35 ‾42 ‾44 ‾45 ‾52 ‾54 ‾55 ‾59 Total

Divide Total by 15 to get average score in Designer category: _____

PROMOTER

‾6 ‾7 ‾9 ‾12 ‾18 ‾19 ‾26 ‾29 ‾37 ‾41 ‾43 ‾47 ‾48 ‾50 ‾57 Total

Divide Total by 15 to get average score in Promoter category: _____

SERVER

‾1 ‾2 ‾8 ‾20 ‾22 ‾25 ‾27 ‾30 ‾31 ‾32 ‾40 ‾46 ‾51 ‾58 ‾60 Total

Divide Total by 15 to get average score in Server category:_____

Copy your totals onto the lines below. Your highest score indicates your primary personality tendency.

_____   _____   _____   _____
Ruler   Designer   Promoter   Server

If you scored over 75 on more than one personality tendency, then your behavior, communication style, and learning style may be fairly flexible. You may be at a level of spiritual maturity where you are able to adjust to changing circumstances.

You may also find that you display one personality tendency in one setting and a different one in another setting. That is why we encourage you to keep in mind a single setting when making decisions on the questions.

If you did not score above 65 on any of the personality tendencies, you are not displaying any particular personality tendency to a significant degree. These are some of the causes of this kind of result:

a) There may be a problem with the test.
b) You may be anxious and "up-tight" over current situations in your life.
c) You may be in transition in your current career, family, or educational circumstances.
d) You may be uncomfortable or unsettled about who you really are.

If you have been unable to define your personality style, we suggest you use the instrument again in two or three months and/or have someone else rate you on the instrument. Above all, allow the Holy Spirit to guide you to truth about yourself.

PACKET: CHAPTER FOUR
Family Communication Game

Introduction:
    This game will teach members of the family how people with different personalities tend to communicate with one another. The goal of the game is better understanding and acceptance of one another's differences. An important preliminary to this game is completion of the personality inventory from chapter three. Once each family member knows the personality styles of the others, he will begin to understand why they sometimes seem to be speaking a different language.
    Object of the Game: Identify the personality after hearing a set of typical communication traits read aloud by another player. The player who gets the most correct answers is the winner.
    Players: Two or more people. If there are four or more, they may want to play as teams.
    Preparing Game Cards: Supplies needed: 3 x 5 index cards, glue, scissors, self-adhesive shelf paper (optional).
    Directions:
    On this packet sheet you will find 20 entries that list a group of communication characteristics typical of one personality type followed by the name of a personality in parentheses. Cut out each square and glue it to an index card.

234

If you want to make a decorative deck of cards, on the other side of the index card affix a colorful piece of self-adhesive shelf paper cut to size.

Rules of the Game: Allow each person in turn to draw a card from the deck. He reads aloud the list of traits and asks the player to his left to name the personality. If the player gives the correct answer, he receives one point and draws a card to read to the person on his left. If his answer is wrong, he loses a turn to read and the next player to his left draws a card. The game can continue as long as desired or until someone receives a total of 21 points. Although young children will be unfamiliar with a few of the words, they will hopefully recognize enough of them to make a decision. In the process, they will be expanding their vocabulary. Be patient with your children and explain what the words mean. This will build family communication skills as much as the game itself.

Other Uses of the Game: As you become more familiar with the concepts in this book, you can add more personality cards on other subjects, such as preferred household chores and careers and methods of learning and listening. Remember that no one person will have all the personality traits listed because each one is an individual. These categories are simply meant to indicate tendencies.

Direct Precise Factual (Ruler)	Enthusiastic Creative Dreamer (Promoter)	Caring Listener Reflective (Server)	Thoughtful Analytical Principled (Designer)
Bossy Forceful Controlled (Ruler)	Expressive Cheerful Animated (Promoter)	Sincere Likes routine Compassionate (Server)	Planner Likes details Asks questions (Designer)
Firm Strong-willed Wants results (Ruler)	Persuasive Open-minded Outgoing (Promoter)	Shy Careful Reserved (Server)	Thorough Restrained Thoughtful (Designer)
Able to lead Productive Opinionated (Ruler)	Talkative Demonstrative Creative (Promoter)	Practical Empathetic Caring (Server)	Orderly Analytical Tactful (Designer)
Competitive Confident Precise (Ruler)	Original Friendly Verbal (Promoter)	Steady Relaxed Gentle (Server)	Conceptual Reserved Avoids eye contact (Designer)

PACKET: CHAPTER FIVE
Problem-Solver Sheet for Single Parents

1. In very objective terms, what is (are) the problem(s)?
2. Who are the family members involved in this problem?
   (a)_____
   (b)_____
   (c)_____
   (d)_____
3. What are the motivational levels, gifts, and personalities of the individuals involved?

Name	Motivational Level	Gifts	Personality
(a)			
(b)			
(c)			
(d)			

4. What motivational level, gifts, and personality would be most ideal in a helper who would desire to assist your family? (Consider both ideal and acceptable qualities.)

   Ideal
   Motivational level_____Gifts_____Personality_____
   Acceptable
   Motivational level_____Gifts_____Personality_____
   Possible Choices
   1. _____
   2. _____
   3. _____
   4. _____

   Persons to ask for confirmation
   1. _____
   2. _____

PACKET: CHAPTER SIX
How to Be a Friend
(A Family Bible Activity)

Introduction:
   The teaching/learning process can be broken down into four steps: **Hear, Learn, Keep, and Do** (based on Deut. 5:1). The following family Bible lesson makes use of those steps. Once you have learned the process, you can adapt it to other Bible lessons you make up yourself, based on subjects like respect for parents, respect for children, how Jesus showed love, or any other theme.

   Be sure to use an actual Bible during these times. This will help your child become familiar with it and assist his spiritual growth. Find a version that is accurate and readable and allow your child to do the reading as much as possible. Before you sit down as a family, read through the lesson yourself and make any preparations necessary. Take time to pray that it will be a productive and enjoyable time for everyone.

HEAR. Read aloud Proverbs 18:24b, John 15:14, and John 13:34-35.

LEARN. Ask the child, "What does the Bible say about being friendly?" After he has paraphrased the verses he just heard (with your help, as necessary), read them aloud again. Help him to memorize Proverbs 18:24b, "There is a friend who sticks closer than a brother."

Discuss how Jesus can be even closer to us than a member of our own family. (Include examples from Scripture of times when He helped people and how He helps us now.) Ask the child to give you examples of friendliness—something he did or someone did for him at home, school, church, etc. Talk about the times you have seen him being friendly to others and praise him for it.

Friendliness Game

In advance, make a written list for yourself of several examples of people being friendly and also being unfriendly. You can draw from personal experience, news stories, Bible stories, or imaginary situations.

When you play the game, tell the child, "I'm going to tell you some stories about people being friendly and people being unfriendly. Every time I give you an example of someone being friendly, stand up. Every time I give an example of someone being unfriendly, sit down."

If the child gives the wrong response, explain quickly but kindly why he was wrong, then go on to the next story. Try to end the game with one of his correct responses.

Once he understands the game, give your child a chance to quiz you, also. His stories may not be sensational, but play along and give him a chance to try his hand at it.

KEEP. Ask your child if he is willing to try to be friendly to others. Encourage him to see it as a gift to Jesus. Remind him that Jesus commanded us to love one another and showed us by acts of love what it means to be friendly. Pray aloud together, taking turns asking God to help you to be friendly. You can start your new commitment to friendliness by a round of hugs for one another.

Role-Playing Game

Introduction:

Sometimes it helps a child to "keep" a lesson he has learned by acting it out in the safety of his home before he enters an awkward situation. You can help him by playing the role first as he watches. In this role-playing game, you will be demonstrating how your child can open a conversation with a new acquaintance.

Directions:
(1) Tell the child that you are pretending he is someone you have never met and you want to be friendly. Before you get close to the child say, as if you were thinking out loud, "I really want to be friendly to this person, but I don't know how to start. I guess I could go up to him and say, 'Hi.'" Walk up, look him in the eye, and say, "Hi. My name is ___. What's yours?"
(2) After he answers, turn aside slightly as if thinking and say, "I need to think

of something nice to say." Then demonstrate small talk such as, "I like the shirt you're wearing" or "Do you want to play ball?" If the child says yes, demonstrate how to continue the conversation. If he says no, show how to gracefully end the conversation, either by offering other options or saying, "Well, maybe another time. Nice talking to you."

(3) Say, "I obeyed Jesus by being friendly to somebody. It feels good to follow His commands, and I know it makes Him happy, too."

(4) Next let your child be the main character, acting out friendliness and speaking aloud as you did. He won't remember everything, but with a little prompting, will come up with quite a bit.

(5) If you wish, have him do the role playing without speaking out loud.

DO. Make a chart with the word "Friendly" at the top. Say, "Every time I see you being friendly, I will put a check on this chart." Then offer a fun activity or other reward that he can anticipate after receiving a certain number of check marks. During the next few days, when you have family devotions together, repeat the main elements of being friendly, such as going up to the person, looking him in the eyes, saying "Hello," introducing yourself, making friendly comments, etc. Talk about new ways to be friendly.

As you watch your child at play, take opportunities to praise him when he does acts of kindness. When he is unkind or selfish (as all children are occasionally) hold him in your lap (if he is still that size) and recall the words you read from the Scriptures.

Each day review the child's progress toward being a good friend and pray with him. Remember the words of Moses: "These words, which I am commanding you today, shall be on your heart; and you shall teach them diligently to your sons and shall talk of them when you sit in your house and when you walk by the way and when you lie down and when you rise up" (Deut. 6:6-7 NASB).

PACKET: CHAPTER SEVEN
"I Love You" Game

Directions:

Object of the Game: It is the purpose of this game to help each player feel good about the way God made him, to help him know who he is in Christ.

Before You Start: It will be helpful, although not necessary, if each person has taken the functional gifts test in chapter two. If you know each person's gifts, list them with his name on a card for use in the game.

Rules of the Game. Have all players seated in a circle or around a table. To start, one individual is chosen as the "Special Person." The player to his left starts the game by saying, "I love you because God loves you and . . .," inserting a gift or talent he has seen in the Special Person.

For example, if Jack is the Special Person and he has the gifts of Mercy and Exhortation, Susie could say to him, "Jack, I love you because God loves you and you like to help people." (This is a typical expresssion of the Mercy gift.)

Dad, the person on Susie's left, could say, "Jack, I love you because God loves you and you have a positive attitude." (This is a typical expression of the gift of Exhortation.)

Scoring: Each time a player comes up with a positive statement, he receives a point. Except for challenges, each player has only one chance to score in each round.

Challenges: If a player makes a statement that someone else thinks is untrue, he can be challenged. The player who disagrees calls out, "Challenge!" He then presents his evidence and the other players discuss whether he is right. For example, Miriam might say, "I don't think Jack had a positive attitude when the coach took him out of the game, so he doesn't have the gift of exhortation." The other players might disagree with the Challenger, saying that Jack recovered and had a good attitude by the time the game was over. Whoever is designated as Judge, usually the parent, will have to make a ruling.

Recovery from a Challenge: If the Judge rules that the Challenger is wrong, the Challenger loses a point. He then has one chance to think of a different positive statement about the Special Person. If the Challenger thinks of a new positive statement, he will regain a half point.

If the Judge rules that the Challenger is right, he is awarded a point. He then has an opportunity to make a different positive statement to replace the one he challenged. This will earn him a second point.

Conclusion of the Game: The game continues with Jack as the Special Person until no one can think of another positive statement about him. At that time, the person to Jack's left becomes the Special Person. Proceeding clockwise, the players begin to make positive statements about the new Special Person. They earn a point for each positive statement they make.

Special Conditions: Young children or those new to the game may repeat something that has already been said by another player.

Scoring: The game continues until one person has scored 10 points. You can use the following scoring sheet to record the points.

Players	1	2	3	4	Points 5	6	7	8	9	10	Total

Personality Profiles

Directions:

The following positive characteristics show up in each personality type at the various motivational levels. The object of the exercise is to find references in the Bible that reaffirm the inherent value of each individual. The first step is for the person to look up his own character traits and write down the verses. The next step is to investigate the positive character traits of other family members.

RULER
(strongest in workmanship qualities)

LEVEL 1	LEVEL 2	LEVEL 3	LEVEL 4
Attentive	Responsible	Resourceful	Diligent
(Heb. 2:1)	(Rom. 14:12)	(1 Sam. 17:50)	(Col. 3:23)

DESIGNER
(strongest in self-control qualities)

LEVEL 1	LEVEL 2	LEVEL 3	LEVEL 4
Cooperative	Obedient	Confident	Peaceable
(Ps. 133:1)	(Jn. 14:23-24)	(Phil 4:13)	(Jn. 16:33)

PROMOTER
(strongest in relationship qualities)

Level 1	Level 2	Level 3	Level 4
Tolerant	Friendly	Sociable	Appreciative
(Rom 14:13)	(Prov. 18:24)	(1 Pet. 3:8)	(1 Thes. 5:18)

SERVER
(strongest in restoration qualities)

Level 1	Level 2	Level 3	Level 4
Sensitive	Gentle	Supportive	Compassionate
(Rom. 12:15)	(2 Tim. 2:24)	(Gal. 6:1-2)	(1 Pet. 3:8)

PACKET : CHAPTER EIGHT
Chore Suggestions

Each home will have numerous chores to be done. Below is a list of possible chores.

1. Feed pet (dog, cat, etc.)
2. Put away hair dryer
3. Clean off stairs
4. Clean own dishes
5. Set table
6. Put away dishes
7. Vacuum carpet
8. Fold clothes
9. Iron
10. Mow lawn
11. Pick up clothes
12. Clean bathroom
13. Polish shoes
14. Weed flower beds
15. Sweep garage
16. Wash mirrors
17. Wash car
18. Set table
19. Edge lawn
20. Open curtains
21. Empty wastebaskets
22. Take garbage out
23. Wind clock
24. Turn out porch light
25. Dust furniture
26. Bundle newspapers

Value Chart
10 points will be given for each weekly task completed
2 points will be given for each daily task completed.
Privileges should be given for a predetermined success rate of about 90 percent each day on the daily chart.
Privileges should be given for a predetermined success rate of about 80 percent for the week, including both the daily and weekly chart.
Special privileges should be given for a predetermined success rate of about 90 percent for the week on the daily and weekly chart.

Privileges — Choose one for each daily success of about 90 percent.
       Choose two for each weekly success of about 80 percent.

1.

2.

3.

4.

5.

6.

Special Privileges — Choose one for each weekly success of about 90 percent.
1.
2.
3.
4.
5.

Chore	Wk. 1	Wk. 2	Wk. 3	Wk. 4	Wk. 5	Remarks
TOTAL						

DAILY CHORES

Chore	M	T	W	TH	F	S	S	M	T	W	TH	F	S	S	Remarks

PACKET: CHAPTER NINE
Problem-Solver Worksheet For Parents

Child's Name:_____
Personality:_____
Motivation Level:_____

1. What is the misbehavior?
2. What corrective strategies have you tried?
3. Have you been successful?
4. What are the general categories for the methods you have tried?
5. Do you believe it is time to use another strategy? Why? Which strategy will you try next?
6. How will you implement the strategy?
7. What character traits are needed to help you solve the problem?
8. If behavior improves, what strategy will you use?
9. If behavior doesn't improve, what strategies will you try?

Child's Behavior Improvement Plan

Name:_____

Date:_____

Area to be improved:

_____will_____

(child)   (Be specific about times, amount, frequency, etc.)

Area to be improved:

_____will_____

(parent)   (Be specific about times, amount, frequency, etc.)

If_____improves,_____will receive the following reward:_____

(behavior)   (child)

If_____does not improve,_____will receive the following consequences:____

(behavior)   (child)

CLEAN ROOM CHART

Name:_____Date:_____

Rules:_____

	MON.	TUE.	WED.	THU.	FRI.	SAT.	SUN.	
Before school								
Before dinner								
Before bedtime								
Before I go out to play								
After my friends leave								Weekly Total
Daily totals								
Comments								

Rewards and compliments:

3 stars each day is Good

4 stars each day is Excellent

5 stars each day is Stupendous

PACKET: CHAPTER TEN
Contract for Setting Behavior Goal

Name:_____

Date_____

I,_____, want to improve my behavior. In order to do so, I am setting the following goals for this week:

1.

2.

3.

4.

5.

I will know I am doing well when the following occurs:

1.

2.

3.

4.

5.

My parents will help me by:

1.

2.

3.

4.

5.

Signed:
(Child)_____
(Parent)_____

Self-discipline Plan
(older children)

What did I do?

What rule did I break?

Why was it a problem?

What is my plan to solve the problem or avoid the problem next time?

_____	_____
Child	Date
_____	_____
Parent(s)	Date

PACKET: CHAPTER ELEVEN
Parental Authority

As you become acquainted with your child's teacher and present her with your suggestions, it is important to keep in mind that God gave parents, not teachers, the responsibility for their child's education. Parents throughout history have used the services of teachers, but it is only recently that parents have stopped participating in the educational process. The following Scripture verses may help redefine your position:

Genesis 2:18-24; 4:1; 33:1-14.
Exodus 20:1-17.
Deuteronomy 6:1-9; 22:13-29.
Psalms 78:1-4; 103:13-14; 127:3-5.
Proverbs 1:1-33; 3:5-12; 23:24-26; 24:3-4; 31:10-31.
Ezekiel 18:1-32.
Mark 5:22-43; 9:14-29.
Luke 15:11-32.
Ephesians 6:1-4
Hebrews 12:7-13.

GOALS
1. What are your general goals for your child's education?
2. What are your specific goals for this quarter? This year?
3. What aspects of life should be included in your child's education? Which should not be included, at least until a later stage?

4. What attitude should the school take about your Christian beliefs? What will you teach your child about dealing with conflicts over his faith? What are his rights?
5. How does the school compare academically to other schools?

MOTIVATIONAL LEVEL
1. What is your child's general motivational level?
2. What situations cause him to regress or advance?
3. How should the teacher deal with the child at this level?

FUNCTIONAL GIFTS
1. What functional gifts does your child possess?
2. How does he demonstrate these gifts?
3. What gifts need to be encouraged?
4. How can the teacher help your child develop these gifts?

PERSONALITY
1. What personality style does your child possess?
2. How will he project his personality in the classroom?
3. What is the most effective way for the teacher to communicate with your child?

DISCIPLINE
1. What is the purpose of discipline?
2. How does your child act when he is angry, inattentive, or rebellious?
3. What techniques should the teacher know about that are the most effective for disciplining your child? Which are ineffective? Which are actually destructive?
4. Which rewards work best for your child?

INSTRUCTION
1. In what environment does your child learn best? Is he easily distracted by other children, or challenged to improve by their presence?
2. What teaching methods are most effective for your child?
3. What learning skills does your child currently possess?
4. How long can your child work on a task?
5. Does your child think globally (concentrates on abstractions and the big picture) or concretely (needs personal involvement with details)?
6. Which method of giving directions is most effective for your child?
7. Which subjects are off-limits for your child? How will you communicate this requirement to the school? Have you explained the reasons to your child and given him alternative instruction?

PHYSICAL AND MENTAL ABILITIES
1. Does your child have any physical, mental, or emotional problems the teacher should know about? Does the school have a policy of instituting counseling or medical treatment (birth control, abortion) without parental consent? How can you protect yourself and your child from anything you consider to be an invasion of family sovereignty?

2. Does your child have any difficulties with hearing, vision, or speech that could affect his ability to perform in class? What adjustments should be made in the classroom to accommodate him?
3. Can your child perform at the same intellectual level as his classmates? If he is at a higher or lower level, what adjustments should be made?
4. How does your child react when under stress? What can the teacher do to help?

UNIQUE EXPERIENCES
1. Has your child had any vacation experiences that the teacher should know about?
2. Has your child had any family experiences that the teacher needs to understand? Has there been death, divorce, abuse, or other trauma?
3. Does your child have any interesting hobbies?

Preparing a Report to the Teacher

Now that you have answered these questions, it is time to summarize the most important elements for the teacher. Since most people don't like to read long reports, and the teacher will probably be skeptical of any parental input, it is up to you to make your presentation brief, interesting, and worthwhile. Remember that you are speaking to the teacher from a position of authority but also speaking the truth in love (Eph. 4:15). Let the fruit of the Spirit (Gal. 5:22-23) be evident in your life as you discuss with the teacher the future of your child.

The following single sheet will help you condense your information for the teacher into the most important categories. You may want to recopy it or submit it the way it is, but be sure you make yourself a photocopy before giving away the final draft of your report.

Most important of all, submit your work to the Lord and let Him guide you. "In everything you do, put God first, and he will direct you and crown your efforts with success" (Prov. 3:6 TLB).

Report to the Teacher

Child's Name   Parents' Names
Phone number   (Home)
                        (Work)
Child's attitudes toward school, teacher, peers

Health, emotional state, and intellectual ability

Child's background, interesting experiences

Gifts and interests

Personality style

Character traits

Best way to motivate my child to excel

Typical misbehavior

Most effective discipline

Most effective instructional methods

Class subjects inappropriate for my child

Additional remarks

Evaluation of Parent-Teacher Conference

Teacher's Name _____ Child's Name _____

Comments before the Conference

1. Why are we having this conference?
2 What is important to achieve?

Comments after the Conference

3. What important information did I obtain about my child, the teacher, the school, etc.
4. Did the conference meet my expectations? Why or why not?
5. Should I do something differently next time?
6. What proved to be beneficial at the conference?
7. What decisions were reached and how will they be implemented?
8. Do I need to follow up on anything? When?
9. Additional insights.

BIBLIOGRAPHY

Adler, M. (1983). *How to Speak, How to Listen.* New York: Macmillan Publishing Company.

Alderfer, C. (1972). *Existence, Relatedness and Growth: Human Needs in Organizational Settings.* New York: Free Press.

Cattell, R.B. and Kline, P. (1965). *The Scientific Analysis of Personality and Motivation.* Baltimore: Penguin Books.

Eysenck, H. (1947). *Dimensions of Personality.* London: Routledge and Kegan Paul.

Haggai, J. (1972). *How to Win Over Worry: A Practical Formula for Victorious Living.* Grand Rapids: Zondervan Publishing House.

Haggai, J. (1979). *How to Win Over Loneliness.* Nashville: T. Nelson.

Kohlberg, L. (1981). *The Philosophy of Moral Development: Moral Stages and the Ideas of Justice.* San Francisco: Harper and Row.

LaHaye, T. (1984). *Your Temperament: Discover Its Potential.* Wheaton, IL. Tyndale House Publishers, Inc.

Magid, K. and McKelvey, C. (1987). *High Risk: Children Without a Conscience.* New York: Bantam Books.

Maslow, A. (1970). *Motivation and Personality.* New York: Harper and Row.

McCarthy, B. (1980). *The 4-MAT System.* Barrington, IL: Excel, Inc.

McDowell, J. (1984). *His Image/My Image.* San Bernardino: Here's Life Publishing, Inc.

McDowell, J. (1985). *The Secret of Loving.* Wheaton: Living Books/Tyndale House Publishing, Inc.

Merrill, D. and Reid, R. (1981). *Personal Styles and Effective Performance.* Radnor, PA: Chilton Book Company.

Prediger, D.J. "A World of Work Map for Career Exploration." *The Vocational Guidance Quarterly,* 24, No. 3 (1976).

Selig, G. (1984). *Training for Triumph.* Shreveport, LA: Huntington House, Inc.